HO]

An Anthology

Westerly Writers' Group

Edition 2020

PREFACE

The Westerly Writers' Group (WWG) is a fellowship passionate about storytelling. Each member, from seasoned editors to first-time authors, brings to the group their own unique life experiences. While writing is a private endeavor, the WWG offers its members an environment of inspiration and thoughtful encouragement.

This anthology is an assortment of essays, fiction, and verse centered on the theme of Homeland. The works extend from a micro view of nature and oneself to a macro view of our nation, world, and humanity.

As it had with every aspect of life in 2020, Covid19 significantly affected the WWG. However, the group persevered, adapted, and continued to assemble, albeit remotely.

Our second goal was to delve into the publication world, which we have discovered is challenging for groups such as we. Despite this, we stretched ourselves and found a way.

Homeland is the Westerly Writers Group's year-long effort to express ourselves and share with one another. We hope that these pieces will ring a true and enjoyable note to you.

Contents

HOMELAND 1
- BELONGING 2
- FIRST LOVE 3
- CRIME JUNKIE 4
- REACH ACROSS AMERICA 6
- GIFT GIVING GRIEVANCES 8
- HOMELAND 10
- SISTERS ON ICE 11
- LITTLE MEXITA 14
- WHO AM I? 16
- MALACHI 17
- A SENSE OF BEING 19
- REGRETS I HAVE A FEW 20
- THERMOSTATS 22
- THE ISLANDS 24
- PRIDE & PREJUDICE 28
- THE AEGEAN AND ME 31
- MOVING THE STATUE 36
- HOME/HOMELAND 42
- HOMELAND AND HERITAGE 44

LOSS 49
- LEAVING 50
- THE PHILOSOPHER 51
- ETERNAL UNHOLY WATER 56
- AN INACTIVE ACTIVIST 58
- KATE 59
- JANIS 62
- WATER 63

EYES ONLY	64
BEN (A.K.A. DAD)	65
OCTOMOM FOR MOTHER'S DAY	68
IT'S FINE	70
SANCTUS	72
MUSIC MAN NO MORE	73
KILLING US SOFTLY	75
MEMBER OF THE FAMILY	77
THE MUGS THAT SAVED OUR MARRIAGE	81
WITH THIS RING	83

NATURE ... 85

THE WILLOW TREE	86
I LOOKED ACROSS THE WATER	87
WATER, WATER EVERYWHERE?	88
POND MUSINGS	90
SEASONAL HAIKUS	92
SURGE	93
SUMMER GUESTS	94
OUTSMARTING COVID	96
HAIKUS	97
THE UPPER ROOM	98
POOL	100
MOMENT TO MOMENT	102
THE REPLY ALLPOCALYPSE	104
A BODY OF WATER	106
STORMS	107
GREAT WATER	109
CAROL'S WRATH	110

HUMANITY ... 116

HOME. LAND. 117
FORGIVENESS 120
THIEF..121
TRUTH 127
SEEKING ASYLUM..128
DELIVERANCE 129
THE EVIL THAT MEN DO..131
NEW YORK STORIES, OR WE ARE ALL IN THIS TOGETHER 132
FAMILY TIES..135
A PERFECT STORM 136
AN OPPORTUNITY TO REIMAGINE THE WORLD.............138

-BIOGRAPHICAL SKETCHES...140
ACKNOWLEGEMENTS..143

HOMELAND

Rise up in unison
Seek rights and liberties
Justice for all peoples.

This domain of mine
Where I rest my head and heart
Among those that I love most.

A land for my home
Unburdened by the tyrants' wills
Nurtures willing souls.

Bradford

BELONGING
Christina Danese

Dante-like, I am midway through my journey. Or a journey. Riding the rails weekly between home and work, I have been living a sort of amorphous existence that is the result of being neither here nor there or both here and there.

Southbound, views of shore towns with their inlets and open spaces fold inward and re-emerge, condensed and congested, as cities. Detrained, I dive headlong into the grind, readjust my pace to match the thrum and throng, and pick things up where I left them last week. I used to find the city enthralling, the way it eternally reinvents itself. Its energy was irresistible and intoxicating. I fed off of it and was renewed by it. I do not know whether it was the city or me that changed but I understood something had shifted when I found myself close to tears as blocks of old walk-ups were razed and replaced with soulless slivers. I used to love the way I could lose or find myself amid my fellow city dwellers, the tourists and those just passing through. At some point that changed and I mostly felt overwhelmed by the crush of so many bodies. The accumulation of years and friendships became not enough. I felt increasingly disconnected from and lost my sense of belonging to the place that had been my home for most of my life.

Northward. Each clack of the wheels on the tracks moves the train forward as the cities and the week shrink, then fall behind in its wake. For a full season, I've observed the concrete and asphalt give way to salt marsh and salt pond. The unfurling land- and seascapes mark my progress towards a house on a rise with views of water and wood. The light, the air, the natural beauty that can take my breath away, invigorate. They have sustained me through the year's-worth of arrivals and departures that have me feeling everywhere and nowhere. The train rides always are a return home; either to the one that was or to the one that is, where a driver's license, a library card and a circle of writers represent my first, tentative steps at wading back into a sense of belonging.

FIRST LOVE
Bernard "Bing" Bartick

It was the year 1958. I was fourteen and a freshman in high school. It was September. I was in love. I did not know what love was, but I was in love anyway. Her locker was across from mine. I saw her twice a day in the morning before school and in the afternoon right after school. I do not know if she ever saw me. I would look over at her hoping that she would not notice me staring at her. Warm feelings flooded every cell of my body. I was high, low, fast, slow, hot, cold, young, old, silly, serious, numb, and gung-ho all at the same time. She was more beautiful than beauty itself. Her face was like the face of a Greek Goddesses' Goddess. She was springtime, she was summertime, and she was fall time. But with her, would I ever spend time? Would she ever be mine?

This daily ritual went on for a whole year. My love grew deeper and deeper. My every thought was about her —except for the school stuff that I had to learn and think about. Did she know that I went to the same school? Did she know that I existed? I had to find out. However, as my love grew, my fear of approaching her also grew. I knew that I had to talk with her----but, but how?

Then came the last day of school. Lockers were being cleaned out. I was at mine. She was at hers. It was now or never. It was time. I, I, I had to do it. I walked over to her. She looked up at me. I stared at her. I said "um, ah, um, ah, oh, um ah." She said," Excuse me." What did you say? My lips could barely move. Strange sounds continued to come out of my mouth. "Um ah, um ah, um ah, oh, oh, oh." She stared at me some more in a quizzical way. I walked away. Perhaps love would come another day.

Epilogue:

We never really dated per-say, but we became good friends and still are today. I had my share of girlfriends in high school but then came September of my first year of college. I was at a freshman welcoming party. I saw another beautiful woman, a Goddesses' Goddesses' Goddess, and this time I approached her right away. Love did come another day. We married four years later. Last year, we celebrated our fifty-third anniversary.

CRIME JUNKIE
Dyann Boudreau

I love true crime. I am a fiend for the deduction, the mystery, and the questions of guilt or innocence. More literary-minded than me might say that true crime as a genre is exploitive, salacious, ugly, and voyeuristic. I say the heart wants what the heart wants.

I'm not alone. Studies show, and yes, there have been studies done on the subject, that women consume far more of these scripted dramas than men. Research has found that women favor stories that show how a potential victim uses a gimmick or trick to avoid or escape an attacker. Women not only enjoy reading and watching these stories, but we also use them as a primer to keep safe.

I know that they made me savvier. You will not catch me being duped by someone on crutches looking for a lost puppy. I now know how to escape a car trunk by finding the glow in the dark latch and to not leave my house key on the ring I give the valet. For sure, true crime has soured me on additional life insurance policies taken out on my behalf.

I began reading true crime stories years ago. I chose a thin tan book from a pile on the coffee table, opened it, and read, "The village of Holcomb stands on the high wheat plains of western Kansas." The words were compelling, disturbing, seductive.

The story was about the Clutters, a simple Kansas family slaughtered for a small portable radio, a pair of binoculars, and less than $50 in cash. My world shifted. They were an ordinary family, with children not much younger than me. The book was *In Cold Blood*. Gone was my belief in the innate goodness of people, but in its place began my love of crime drama.

True crime is at its best when it delivers an ample supply of intrigue and suspense. A hint at the prurient is a bonus. For the audience, the plots are endless. There are family annihilators, sex crimes, children who kill for an inheritance, even parents who kill to rid themselves of liability. Every story comprises original characters, and each true drama begins somewhere new and ends somewhere unexpected. Who thought O. J. Simpson would be found innocent? Who knew that they would acquit Robert Blake?

One criticism of the true-crime genre is that it skews the public's perception. The mostly female fanbase fears falling victim despite statistics proving otherwise. Most true crime dramas deliver a tidy ending with the perpetrator caught and convicted. But, almost half of the murders committed in the US go unsolved.

While it might be justified to say that true crime misleads the public about the legal process, I say I know what my heart wants.

REACH ACROSS AMERICA

Carol Maynard

Plymouth Rock
They took the rock to be their own
Though well populated
With our native friends.
New London, Newport, New England, New York
The beginning of a nascent nation,
Started here, in the Pilgrim's new home

Heartland
Endless rows of wheat and corn
Driving, driving, horizon in sight.
Sameness, flatness, wholeness.
Shall we watch the grass grow?
'Til our jeans are worn?
'Til the sheep are shorn?

Sweet Bayou
Plodding, humid, stifling heat
Wild festivity in syncopation,
Hospitality, gracious living.
Spanish mosses in breezy sway,
Raining frogs
Time stands still, as strangers meet.

Rocky Mountains
Bright skies, wide open spaces,
Falcons, hawks, golden eagles,
Lofty heights, lazy circles.
Dark red clay, steep cliffs rising,
Touching blue
Breathing deep, steady paces.

Shining Pacific
The coast stretches long and wide,
Winding roads with awesome vistas
Haciendas in Spanish style,
A legacy to days gone by.
Hollywood, Malibu, Fresno, 'Frisco
Golden glow at eventide.

GIFT GIVING GRIEVANCES
Jane Barstow

My husband bought me a five-speed bicycle and himself a ten-speed bicycle for an engagement present since I didn't want a ring. It was not an auspicious beginning to our gift-giving history.

"Aren't we planning to ride together," I asked, somewhat unkindly.

"Well, that's the general idea," he responded.

"And which of us has the stronger legs," I continued.

"I suppose I do," he acknowledged.

After a pregnant pause, he smiled somewhat sheepishly, "I guess you need as many gears as I do if you hope to keep up with me."

I thought that I actually needed more gears than he did but was pleased when he at least promised to exchange my bike for a ten-speed just like his.

Other gift-giving fiascos followed over the years. There was the Fredrick's of Hollywood negligee which I never figured out how to wear and found rather ridiculous; I much preferred my baggy t-shirts. There were countless outfits in the wrong size, dozens of pieces of jewelry I would never wear recommended by store clerks, and truly bizarre objects d'art that soon began to accumulate in our basement.

As our girls got older and my husband asked their advice, the gifts got noticeably better. At some point, we had the good sense to replace gift-giving with donations to our favorite non-profit organizations. What a relief.

There was still the problem, however, of extended family gift-giving. Christmas Eve at my in-laws meant lots of wrapping paper and lots of junk most of which ended up in the trash within a few months. One December I brightly suggested we exchange homemade gifts. My husband spent hours on lovely macramé plant hangers and belts, I made colorful ties and scarves. I actually looked forward to the reception I was sure our crafts would receive and hoped my sisters-in-law would reciprocate with their famous cookies and handmade earrings. How wrong I was.

Fortunately, I have forgotten or repressed many of these traumatic holiday moments. So, let me conclude with the Christmas gift most beloved by my daughters despite my husband's attempt to veto its acquisition. Perhaps I was partly motivated by a spirit of gift-giving revenge knowing that a kitten might well trigger allergies he claimed to have.

It was easy to choose the "right" kitten at our local shelter given his shiny calico coat and the way he clung purring to my sweater when I gingerly took him out of his cage. A cat-loving friend agreed to hide him until Xmas morning when I snuck out just minutes before the girls awoke and brought him home in a ribbon covered carrier.

Sarah cried upon seeing the breathing package beneath the tree, "But you told us we couldn't have a cat because of Daddy." I simply smiled in response.

Amanda immediately opened the carrier and began cuddling the tiny bundle of fur in her arms.

My husband never did break out in hives though he did occasionally sneeze to remind us of his sacrifice. And Marshmallow, as the girls named him, kept us happily distracted on gift-giving occasions for years to come as he played with the wrappings of the countless boxes of unappreciated stuff.

HOMELAND
Al Clemence

My home is on a wooded knoll, scant miles from the sea.
Protected by an island and sheltered by a sandy cape.
It faces just east of north and warns of storms that threaten me.
A tiny piece of land, many miles from where the continent divides.
It is where I am often found and where I most like to be

My home is in a village, nestled by the sea.
Protected by its past from a future yet to be
Guided less by purpose and more by whim.
It measures time with little care, for the changes that will greet it there.
It is where I am often found and where I wish to be.

My home is anchored to a giant land that binds vast oceans to its shores.
Protected by those who honor truth and justice under laws.
It is but a station on the journey that I'm on.
A place where I may stop to rest before I go, again, away.
A place where I shall plot the course that brings me home to stay.

I stand astride a giant sphere racing through the night.
Protected by forces yet to be imagined, then proven to be right.
My Captain is known by many names, for me he has but one.
He guides me among foreign worlds, as we wander with the sun.
I wonder why it is, that here, we cannot share the mysteries of Earth.

I have chased the sun across the sky, to catch its waning light.
I have waited in quiet darkness, for the waning of the night.
Searched the dawn for signs my land was near.
Felt the joy, when with the morning light it did appear.

My home is more than just a place by a shining sea.
It is where my journeys began.
The place that calls me back again.
It is where I will be found and where I most want to be.

SISTERS ON ICE
Eric Maynard

Applause. Camera phones flash, glimmering arena seats, as if from a stationary mirror ball.

Thousands of children, girls, cheer for Princess Kookoo. Princess Kookoo, beloved animated character, glides across the ice, accompanied by intonements from the PA system: "Ladies and gentlemen, young and old, the star of our show…Waldo Mersch's Fantastical Princess Kookoo and Her Enchanted Ice Spectacular!"

Her skates sharp, her body trim and loaded with muscle memory.

Greta Soreen is Princess Kookoo today. And tomorrow, both matinee and evening. And for the entire East Coast run of the Ice Spectacular. Greta trained to be a professional figure skater since the age of four. She was a hopeful for the 2018 Winter Olympics. An ankle injury while preparing for the Olympics left Greta an immediate has-been at twenty-five years old.

Greta, relegated to wearing a form-fitting mock-up of Princess Kookoo.

Frilly skirt. Light blue trim dress. Skintight flexible cloth underneath.

A reflection of Princess Kookoo. A flesh and blood stand-in, a role model, an idol of millions of American girls.

Strobe lights tickle the ice-covered arena floor.

Greta smiles, arms outstretched, skating, soaring across the ice.

Ice shavings, flakes, fly from her skates.

Flakes settle on a mirror.

Sasha, Greta's younger sister, leans over the gleaming porcelain sink surface. Sasha, sheltered, hunkers down in Greta's dressing room lavatory. She hovers above the sink, shifting, searching for balance, compact mirror in one hand and rolled-up dollar bill in the other.

Sasha snorts a line of cocaine off the mirror. Sweat beads collect around her forehead.

She rubs her left nostril, drawing cocaine further down her nasal passage. Swallowing, and an exhale.

Sasha looks up, staring for a moment. Her sister's thick coat, Greta's coat, suspends, hooked on the bathroom stall door.

"Princess Kookoo's coat…" Sasha laughs to herself.

She knows Greta's secret.

If only they knew, she thinks. If only those adoring girls knew about Greta's sickness, of her fear of eating. A fear that she would lose her figure, that nourishment might deform her. That Greta would not be able to fit into Princess Kookoo's outfit. That the coat would be too tight.

Perfect Greta, Sasha thinks.

Her smile fades.

Sasha looks at her likeness in the compact. She sees drawn blood-shot eyes, the dried-out remnants of promise.

Sees her earlier self, a child, running after Greta, ice skates tied together, slung over her shoulder. Sasha wants to practice, too. Wants to practice with Greta, entertain like Greta, to be with Greta. She wants the attention of coaches, of parents, the attention her sister receives as if inherited. Just like Greta.

Sasha was told, "No, you are too little..."

No, no, no...Your sense of balance stinks. You are not meant for skating. Let's find something better suited for Sasha...

She's so quiet...so shut off, so shut down...what can we do with her?

Her parents' voices. Now, they sounded like one voice, Sasha's voice.

Sorry...screwed up again...sorry...

The drugs, the alcohol, the rehabs.

Shut off...shut down...

The false starts at college. At employment: Costco, house cleaning. Finally, Personal Assistant to her sister, Princess Kookoo.

A last-ditch effort to help poor, lost Sasha...what a good sister Greta is to hire her...

"And now, our journey into the Ice Palace of Mirrors," calls out the announcer.

Sasha hears the proclamation, muffled, in the bathroom.

It finally occurs to her. "Oh shit," she says. Her cue. Thumb and forefinger, she rubs the remaining cocaine on her upper and bottom gums. She shoves the compact in her jeans pocket.

Sasha runs out, stumbles, floundering, cradling Greta's coat. Sasha runs past the stage crew, the sound technicians, the cables and immense Princess Kookoo-themed stage risers. Runs to catch her sister.

Behind a set of risers, concealed from the audience: Greta waits. Arms envelop her chest, her hands clasp her elbows, her face red.

"Jesus, Sasha," she says. "Where the hell were you? I'm freezing."

"I...I..." Sasha's teeth clamp tight.

"C'mon." Greta grabs at the coat. "It's the one thing I count on. From you. One thing."

Sasha let go of Greta's coat. A bead of blood forms in Sasha's left nostril and trickles down.

Greta shifts her gaze to Sasha's nose. "Sasha…what the shit, Sasha?!"

As the coat leaves Sasha's grasp, she catches the blood droplet streaking toward her lips.

"Sorry," she says.

"Sorry," Greta repeats her sister. "Sorry…me, too…sorry…Sasha, this keeps happening…"

"I'm sorry," Sasha says.

Crimson tears congeal.

Sasha leans into her sister. Greta shoulders the weight, balanced for both of them.

Coagulation.

LITTLE MEXITA
Dyann Boudreau

The phone app controlling my thermostat was not working this morning. I had to run downstairs to turn up the heat, feeling like a caveman out scavenging for firewood. After I hopped back under the covers, it occurred to me technology has made our lives easier, faster, and more self-indulgent.

Apps like Waze, Skype, and Venmo have made travel, communication, even bill paying almost effortless. But before computers and the apps that run on them came along, life was fine.

I can recall, almost half a century past, time spent at my grandparents' lake house. One aunt's souvenirs from a Mexican vacation peppered the cabin, so we dubbed it Little Mexita. Rustic Little Mexita lacked almost every comfort and convenience, but for us, it was grand.

It was a tiny cabin for a large family. My grandparents had seven children, so the house saw a continuous ebb and flow of cousins; aunts, uncles, and unexpected tag-a-longs.

I was the youngest and there were so many relatives I didn't always know, or care, who belonged to whom. We knew each other's names and a nebulous idea of where each of us hung on the family tree. And honestly, that was enough.

The three-bedroom cabin held two sets of double bunk beds and a few army surplus cots that would be set up each night. This allowed for many secret, whispered discussions among us cousins.

During the day we would picnic in the pine groves or sneak over to peek into the houses left empty for the summer. But most of the time we were in the lake. We had an old orange raft to paddle and rubber inner tubes for carefree drifting. There was a dock to jump from and lie on to dry. In the back garden, my grandfather had built a tall river stone fireplace. There we would fry up the sunfish and pickerels we caught.

Behind the cabin, under the sugarberry trees, there sat an old well. We would pour a pail of water from the lake down the metal spout to prime the suction valve. Then one of us would furiously pump the metal well handle until the water gurgled its way up the pipe. To us kids, it seemed almost wizardry.

We would stay out until dusk when the mosquitos chased us indoors. At night we played cards and board games while the parents sat and talked out on the screened porch. It might sound provincial but for us, it was brilliant.

The digital revolution has given us a host of advancements. I enjoy having the house toasty warm first thing in the morning. But life before the technology boom was enjoyable too. The takeaway here is that logging off does not mean you're missing out. What matters is spending time with others. Live the experience: Hike a trail, row a canoe, have a picnic. Do it for the fun of it, not for Instagram karma.

WHO AM I?
Bernard "Bing" Bartick

I am a child of the Universe

A resident of a Galaxy

An occupant of a Solar System

A tenant of the Earth

A dweller of a Continent

A citizen of a Country

A denizen of a State

An addressee of a Town

An indweller of a Village

A member of a Family

A lodger of a Self

A portion of the Human Race

MALACHI
Mel Jolly

Of my four uncles on my mother's side of the family, one uncle, in particular, had such a uniqueness about him that he left me with life-long indelible memories. Uncle Malachi was the youngest male of the nine children my grandparents raised.

When I was growing up, he was the uncle who often would just 'pop in' to see how things were going, invariably arriving with a bag of donuts or sweet rolls in hand. He would fetch himself a glass of milk, perch at the dining room table, and commence eating his 'snack.' I, on the other hand, was like the proverbial cat watching a canary: It usually did not take long for my uncle to drift off into sleep, my signal to reach for a donut or jellyroll! I would creep over to the table, and quietly attempt to open the bag of goodies without making any noise. Without fail, every time I would get my hand just into the bag, my uncle's voice bellowed out "I see you, boy," and then he would laugh.

For years I watched my uncle's pattern of falling asleep within minutes after he sat down and simply assumed, he was tired. One day, my grandfather asked me to ride along with Uncle Malachi to the downtown post office. I never had been anywhere with my uncle behind the wheel, but I was certain my grandfather's reason for telling me to go along was to ensure Uncle Malachi didn't fall asleep while he was driving.

Minutes into our journey, we approached a traffic light turning yellow. My uncle slammed on the brakes, causing us to skid into the middle of the intersection. At the same time, he turned the wheel and slid across the seat, pinning me up against the passenger's door. There we sat in the middle of the road, me terrified that we were about to be blindsided by another car, and Uncle Malachi trying to get himself back to his side of the front seat. All the while, he was trying to rationalize to me that the brakes 'must be faulty.' The remainder of our journey that day, while safe and uneventful, was in complete silence.

A few months after the infamous trip to the post office, there was a family gathering. I wasn't paying much attention to the adult conversation until I heard someone talking about Uncle Malachi and his Golden Gloves Boxing career. The story everyone was giggling about was the match in which my uncle was sent to his neutral corner after knocking down his opponent in the First Round. Apparently, the referee counted as far as 'Eight,' at which point the opponent got up from the canvas, went over to Uncle Malachi, who was standing in the corner with his arms over the ropes but sound asleep, and knocked him out!

I have no idea when — or if — Uncle Malachi ever was diagnosed with Narcolepsy. I do know his 'naps' never were a deep sleep, and they occurred when he was sedentary, or at rest, even for a very short time. Of all my uncles though, he was the one I spent the most time with; he was the one I truly enjoyed the most. Uncle Malachi never went to college, and he didn't have a very successful career, but he always was helpful and understanding. He never was too busy to lend a hand when my other uncles were preoccupied with being popular and important figures in our community.

I always have remembered and been thankful for everything my Uncle Malachi did to encourage me to believe in myself, to follow my path rather than chase a crowd. I saw in my uncle a man who wouldn't give up: he had three morning paper routes and a car wash created out of a garage, yet he still studied the Bible to become a better spiritual leader and found time to spend with the nephew kid who had neither a mother nor a father in his life.

Reflecting back on Uncle Malachi, I realize that perhaps he is at least part of the reason I enjoy trying to help kids through coaching. It all stems from the guy who never gave up, regardless of the odds or obstacles set before him. I can never repay him for helping me along the way, but I certainly can be grateful for his being there for me.

A SENSE OF BEING
Al Clemence

There is a shared sense of being that binds us one to another.
That binds a place to a distant place, a bird to a bee and you to me.
I see it in a glance. I see it in a smile.
I hear it in a whispered breath and in the sounds of a song.
It sparkles for a moment then darts away.
Try as I may to hold it near, I cannot make it stay.
It was there in Flanders fields when poppies bent to gentle winds.
It may be there still.
It lingers with the tiny bird that waits for the one that lies broken on the windowsill.
It is the promise of something that yet may be, to which I am bound.
Try as I may, I cannot turn my steps until it too has gone away.

REGRETS I HAVE A FEW
Dyann Boudreau

The next time you're cringing on a past poor decision, try to consider it on the universe's spectrum of poor decisions. Burt Reynolds took a pass on playing both James Bond and Indiana Jones. One publisher rejected Harry Potter because it was too long. Tiger Woods' dalliance cost him $750 million. And Excite.com turned down an offer to buy Google for less than $800K, which is now worth, no kidding, $1 trillion dollars. I wonder if the spouse of whoever nixed that deal ever brings it up at the supper table.

My own regrets, placed in that context, are far less significant. Yet, late at night, most often when I'm wrestling with sleep, the lame-brained stunts from my past will come back to haunt me.

I should not have taught my cousin Janice that flipping the bird was the fourth sign of the cross. Mea culpa, I regret stealing those purple pipe cleaners from the art class in second grade. While I'm not entirely sure that it was stealing, Sister Hortense was pretty goddamn clear about it.

And I still rue the day that I intervened between Charlie and that bully. Charlie's my younger brother by five years, not such a big difference once you're past twenty. But it is virtually generational between the ages of ten and five.

What happened with that was this. It was the summer after fifth grade. Me and my friend Kelly were playing in her backyard when Kelly's little sister came running over to us and blurted out, "Charlie's over at the O'Brien's and-and he's crying, and there's a bully picking on him and he's crying and they're being mean to him." She was nearly in tears herself.

Kelly and I double-timed it across the four lawns that separated her house and the O'Brien's. We pushed through their back gate to find what appeared to be the aftermath of a minor league skirmish.

In one corner of the yard stood the O'Brien twins, boys one grade ahead of me. With them was a third boy I didn't recognize. This new kid was taller than the twins. He wore a blue and white striped rugby shirt with a popped collar, and he had a string of puka beads around his neck.

Closer to the fence was my brother Charlie. He was ugly crying, his little face streaked with dirt and snot and sweat. In his corner were his buds, TJ and Spud. TJ and Spud were examining the ground and shuffling their feet, offering as much help as could be expected from two five-year-old's.

"Charlie, Charlie," My arms wrapped around his little quivering shoulders, "Okay, okay, what happened, are you all right, who did this?"

Between gasping sobs, Charlie raised his arm, gave his nose a long swipe on his sleeve, then pointed towards Puka Beads. At that moment, something inside me snapped and for the first time in my life - and honestly, the last - I was completely blinded by rage.

With no definitive plan, I turned from Charlie and stormed across the yard. Maybe if the white-hot brew of anger and adrenaline boiling in my brain had cleared for just one second, I might have scrubbed the mission. But halfway across the yard, me and Puka Beads locked eyes, and I saw in his more bewilderment than bravado. It cemented my resolve.

When the distance between me and Puka was just about closed, I took one last step and planted my foot right up into his goolies. He went down cupping his groin and the O'Brien boys, in unison, sucked in air.

I turned and double-timed it back to Charlie. I didn't dare turn around. As I took him by the arm to lead him home, Charlie looked up to me, then sobbed out, "Not him."

Footnote: I recognize this as not my proudest moment and my regret is sincere. I never got in trouble for this either. Maybe because Charlie and I kept it secret, or maybe because I'm a girl. Either way, for both me and Charlie, it was a lesson in looking before you leap.

THERMOSTATS
Phoebe Huang

My daughter and I like to check out our happiness thermostats. On a scale of 1 to 10, she figures her normal setting is between 6 and 7. She can get up to 8 and 9 but rarely falls below 5. I have similar settings. My husband hovered between 4 and 5, but could, with great food, jump up to a 9 momentarily.

Those were the very best times with him. Some spouses say they love their husbands for their minds, their sense of humor, the companionship, etc. I loved Sam's enjoyment of good food. His "it doesn't get better than this" smile would erupt when he tasted something absolutely delicious. And "absolutely delicious" came around primarily when he cooked it.

Sam liked to say that anyone could become a good cook. I proved him wrong, despite good faith efforts and a B.A. in chemistry - something Sam claimed could only be a bonus in the kitchen. One gap, for sure, is that I lack any internal food database: I don't instinctively know which flavors go with what. Worse, I have no food memory either.

We can credit baloney sandwiches with the discovery of Sam's talent - that is, one too many baloney sandwiches. His graduate school roommate provoked a revolt by serving these up every time it was his turn to "cook."

With practice and natural talent, Sam made everywhere we lived "the house of good food." Where some kids can count on new toys, sports tickets to boost their popularity, our kids had their dad in the kitchen. From time to time, out of a misguided sense of burden-sharing, I would offer to cook dinner. Our kids' friends knew to verify who was cooking before heading over.

He invented many dishes, simple and not, that the three of us who remain, catch ourselves reminiscing "Do you remember when Dad....?" One memory was less winsome. Sam set a large pan of duck fat to cool on the back steps leading to the garden. This was fat rendered from roasting two ducks.

Someone opened the back door, and Rufus, our eighty-pound golden retriever ran out, splat into the pan, turning it over on himself. I have suppressed what it took to clean all that fur (think of ducks caught in an oil slick.) All I'll say is that washing Rufus in boiling water would have been easier. Only, like most goldens, Rufus was just too lovable. And, he enjoyed morsels from the table.

One creation, Lap Cheong and eggs, is a reason I married Sam. For two servings, he would cut a link of Chinese sausage into 1/8-inch rounds. These he rendered in a non-stick saucepan until the fat in the slices became translucent. He added a handful of sliced mushrooms, along with two minced scallions until the mushrooms partly cooked through. Finally, four beaten eggs seasoned with some salt and pepper (not too much salt for the sausages are flavored) were stirred in until the desired consistency. We liked the eggs creamy. A perfect brunch dish, guaranteed to make him or her, yours.

Another simple dish no one can resist: roasted potato wedges. Cut 3 potatoes, russets or sweet, into lengthwise wedges, like home fries. Season, pop into a quart Ziploc, moisten to taste with oil of your choice, then microwave for 5 minutes. Lay wedges, skin side down, on a greased baking sheet and broil until lightly browned and crisp. Can take 10-15 minutes with turning.

Two other dishes we lost when we lost Sam. One is a filet mignon - so tender and flavorful, ordering a restaurant filet is no longer possible. The key ingredient was a "demi-glace" that Sam put together from some leftover oxtail stew. What went into the stew? Who knows? Sam never wrote recipes down.

The other dish began with the freshest prawns. Then what? The flavors were too complex and wedded to pick out. Something red went in. Five minutes later, out came a dish so luscious; shrimp will also never be the same.

The 9's and 10's we hit on the happiness thermostat when Sam cooked for us will also be just a memory.

THE ISLANDS
Joe Taylor

The main island, "Mason's Island," is just off the mainland, and connected to another islet by a narrow causeway. This islet has a small oratory on it with a rocky ridge running down to the water. An old priest lives there in a house and says mass daily. I met Cathleen out there one Sunday after church. Friends introduced us and the rest is history. She is tall, fair, and lovely. We got along well together, and with our mutual friends. Cathleen and I were married two years later in the chapel on the small island, where we had met.

I had bought an acre of land on the north end of the big island and we planned to live there together. The plot was near an outcropping called Pine Point. The builder had to excavate down ten feet to reach solid rock to build on. This was a pain. As the men neared the rock below, they came upon many flintlike fragments with sharp edges that looked like arrowheads. The site was quickly cordoned off with thin rope and stakes. We did not know what to do next.

Cathleen and I were friends with a local librarian at the time. She and the police decided to get the local state archeologist to come down and look at what had been unearthed. The archeologist told us that this was likely an old ancient burial grave from the fourth century. There are also several Ogham standing stones dating from that period on the mainland. The inhabitants back then might row out to the island in the summer and set up camp to fish in the river. There were many, wild berry thickets there too. Most likely, they buried their dead there also. Well, this put a whole different spin altogether on the story. Our plot was now holy ground for a variety of interest groups, not to mention the Irish government and there were New Age cults around too.

Needless to say, this put the kibosh on our plans, and the money spent on the foundations was lost! We did get some of it back from the state though, and we bought another plot about five miles away. Before it was all cordoned off. I squirreled away a few of the artifacts for myself and put them into my car boot until we built the new house, it was our land after all! We built the new house within a year and moved on. The state, of course, made a meal out of the grave investigation and cataloging the artifacts found there. In the end, they didn't dig deeper or wider since the trench we had come upon was shaped by a crucible-like formation in the sandstone and likely unique.

As time went on, we had two boys there, Declan and Bobby. Cathleen and I were both teachers in local schools so were never that far from home. The islands are a lovely place, set near a bend on the River Bandon in County Cork. The Bandon rises in the nearby Shehy mountains, flowing through Dunmanway down to the Atlantic at famed Kinsale. You are near civilization but can get away from it easily too. It was an idyllic place to raise the boys. There was ample fishing in the nearby river and a deep swimming hole out the island. Also, a small yacht club where the boys learned to sail in small dinghies. Cathleen loved to explore around with the boys in the summer. They often wandered among the fields and stone walls and through old graveyards. The winters were damp, of course, but that's Ireland for you.

One year, we were in our great room in the evening with a fire burning in the fireplace, when Cathleen said to me,

"Do you feel that little tremor?" I assumed it was vibrations from a train across the way going over the railway bridge to Cork City. The trains would pass by several times a day.

"No, it's more than that. Maybe there is a minor earthquake in the area. It happens sometimes as the sandstone rock settles occasionally." But I had felt it too and it was very queer. It happened again from time to time, but we got used to it.

Then though, the keening started at night. It was like the banshee that my mother had told me about when I was a child. When someone was about to die, the banshee, a ghost, would circle over the house of the sick person and making a terrible, mournful screeching sound. Thankfully, the boys were in bed at that time, but we were both shaken by it.

It didn't happen again until a month later. This time we had neighbors in the house for drinks. It was a tradition on the island to host your neighbors at the time of the Winter Solstice. The boys heard it first. They thought it was great fun. But Cathleen was distraught, what with the neighbors in the house and the time of year. The neighbors felt it too and were very jumpy. Nobody wanted to talk about it. They whispered quietly amongst themselves and stole away furtively earlier than was customary. No doubt it was a big scandal in the town, on the mainland too!

We were frightened and afraid of what had happened. The boys were shaken too, no doubt affected by our own evident fear. The next day, we went out to the priest on the islet and asked him to say mass and help us get rid of any spirits that might be in our house. His name is Father Tom Hoar, from Skibbereen, a nice man and warmhearted too. He agreed to help us, and we settled on the next Thursday.

On that morning with the sun shining, we invited all of the neighbors back to the house for the casting out. The water was dead calm on the day. The neighbors stood outside. We had invited them. Then the priest, in all his regalia, walked into the house and sprinkled holy water in every room and over us and the boys. When it was done, everyone filed into the great room and had breakfast. We were happy in our minds again. The spirits were cast out and we could rest and sleep with easy minds. We all went to the seaside for Good Friday and had a great time there together.

At Easter, though it started again, but only worse than before. We decided to send the boys to their cousins for a while and talked about selling the house. We could not go on like this after all. We talked about our predicament with close friends, the ones who had introduced us back then. They said,

"We don't want you to go, we love you."

"I'm demented with this and can't keep doing it anymore." Said Cathleen. Cathleen's friend, Mary, tried to calm her and said,

"Let's talk to the librarian again, she might have some thoughts."

We did as Cathleen suggested. The librarian knew of a Celtic sect near Belgooly. They had a domicile there and were respectful of the ancient traditions. Maybe they had a priest who could provide insight where ours couldn't? She contacted them for us, and their priestess came down the next day with a group of her followers. She walked the land with us and chanted hymns and lit foul-smelling poultices. She came back again a fortnight later and did it again to be sure. We were not expecting much from this Pagan cleansing, and sure enough, it started again a few days after. Within a fortnight we put the house up for sale and settled on new schools for the boys.

The very night before we were about to close on the sale of the house, I was at home and reminiscing on our time on the island. The highs and the lows. The great times with the boys and the torture we had been through. It reminded me that I still had the ancient arrowheads from the excavations on the land we had initially planned to build on. They were no use to me now. I still had them. They were in our cellar, under the new house. I moved them there when we moved in, taking them from the old car boot. A crazy thought flashed across my brain. Could this have anything to do with our troubles? Cathleen was there with me and we talked about it for a while. We were beaten down then and in despair. I convinced her, though, to put the closing back a month on the off chance. The buyers were pissed off, of course, and we had no good reason to tell them other than a haunted house. I gathered up the fragments that day and brought them to the priestess and told her our full story. She was furious at my desecration of the ancient graves.

Eventually, though, she took them and agreed to bring them to the State archeologist for proper keeping. God knows if she did. Thankfully, we never heard any more of that!

Nothing happened at the house for the next four weeks, so we extended the closing another month. At that stage, the buyers were raging and dropped out of the deal altogether. We went on like this, month after month. Eventually we told the priest about the Celtic casting-out and the relics and he cursed us mightily twice, once for stealing and the second time for the Pagan exorcism, which was blasphemy in his eyes

We are still living in that house, living month to month and hoping nothing changes. The boys are grown now and living in the city, but they come back often to our haunted house on the island.

PRIDE & PREJUDICE
Mel Jolly

I was taken aback when the coach told our college basketball team we would be going south to play two universities located in the Deep South. The year was 1962; there had been innumerable displays of racial unrest throughout the United States, so the thought that I might be going into the lions' den was terrifying.

After the team meeting, the coach pulled me aside and asked how I felt about the impending trip. Since I was born and raised in Indiana, I really didn't have much knowledge about the south; my source of information was limited to what I had read in the newspapers or seen on the nightly television newscasts. I told the coach that if the rest of the team was agreeable with my being with them, I certainly was okay. The coach responded that he didn't want me to feel abandoned because of my color; he wanted me to be part of the team.

The first day we were in the south, we were walking along a beach when a "white" girl yelled out 'Hey, Mel Jolly,' as she sped by in a dune buggy. My teammates looked over at me with expressions of shocked surprise, as they tried to figure out how I could possibly know someone this far south. Meanwhile, the dune buggy turned around, came back, and stopped next to me. The girl introduced herself and explained she was from Indiana; her high school had played mine, so she recognized me from having seen me play basketball. I definitely felt a sense of pride to be recognized and acknowledged, but I also was fearful about the possibility of being seen by someone who would look upon this white girl conversing with me with more prejudiced eyes. I quickly introduced my teammates, who were all white, to the girl, and then moved as far away from the group as I could.

That night, I heard my teammates talking about sneaking out after curfew, so I decided I would go out as well, but by myself. When I called a taxi company from the payphone across the road from where we were staying, I gave the address of my location. The reality of prejudice reared its head again when the dispatcher asked if I was white or colored. I told him I was colored, to which he snapped back that I would have to call a colored cab company, then abruptly hung up. The interaction caused me to wonder if maybe I shouldn't bother to dress for the upcoming game the next day. I spent the night mulling over in my mind what Jesse Owens or Jackie Robinson would have done when faced with a similar situation.

The next morning, all seemed to be well: I had breakfast together with my teammates – in the same place, at the same time. I didn't get hassled by anyone, so my confidence improved, and I felt a sense of pride in knowing I actually was going to play basketball at Stetson University that night. As we warmed up on the court before the game, who should appear courtside, but the girl from the beach. I really had no idea how to react: With pride toward once again being acknowledged, this time on the court of the opposing team – or – worried about being subjected to a display of prejudice, because a white girl sought me out in front of a packed arena. Remember: This was 1962 in the Deep South!

I was the first Negro to ever play against the Stetson University team on their home court. That reflection alone made me nervous about playing, and I felt I was off my game. Imagine my surprise when I had the ball and the crowd applauded. I made only one basket that night, but my sense of pride was overwhelming when I realized I was being given a standing ovation. As I sat on the bench after the coach took me out of the game, an unexpected thought ran through my mind: Even though I played on the Number 1 ranked high school team in the nation, I never received the attention I had just felt on this court – the court where I almost had been too afraid to play. I was accustomed to noisy, cheering crowds; however, what stunned me was my sudden understanding that this audience simply appreciated a good basketball game – it didn't matter what the players looked like. I was scrutinized on the basis of my playing ability, not my color. No doubt my initial anxiety affected my play that night; nonetheless, a couple 'spectacular' passes probably compensated for my lack of baskets during the game!

The next day, the sports section of the local paper headlined that history had been made at the game the night before. The article recognized my play during the game and how welcoming the crowd had been toward me, as well as my response to the crowd in return.

I swelled with pride as I read that article, but I have never forgotten how my coaches and teammates supported me on that trip. Coming from Indiana, they were no more prepared for the challenges prejudice might present than I was. The irony though, was that in 1962, I was treated better down south, by strangers, than I was on my home campus, where I might as well have been invisible.

THE AEGEAN AND ME

Jane Barstow

From Soaking Tubs to Oceans, from Canals to Seas, from Rivers to Gulfs, Bays and Sounds: bodies of water have been essential to my identity, political education, and well-being. I grew up in Chicago with Lake Michigan as my lodestar. My sense of direction developed from Chicago's easy geography: The Lake and its playgrounds to the East, the wealthy suburbs to the North, the famous museums to the South, and the cool shops and neighborhoods to the West. My first crush at the age of 12 was on the artist who painted my portrait during our annual family vacation to South Haven. My first near-death experience was at the age of 16 when I slipped through the ice while stupidly chasing friends across the not so frozen lake.

Each of Chicago's beaches had its own special vibe and social caste. Suburban beaches were either privately owned or limited to town residents, though rebellious teenagers managed to walk from one to the next in search of the best parties thrown by the "best" crowds. I learned to swim, sail, play volleyball and drink on Lake Michigan. I suspect many of my friends lost their virginity on its shores, though I did not. I did lose a different kind of innocence, as the shoreline's social divisions taught me my place within its hierarchy.

I left Lake Michigan behind as I grew older, went away to college and started to travel the world, always in search of new adventures and beautiful beaches. Both sides of the Atlantic offered memorable experiences from France to the Bahamas and both sides of the Pacific from Japan to Costa Rica. The great, short-lived romance of my life occurred on the Mekong River. Years later, my rather dismal honeymoon was spent on a cold and rainy island in Lake Ontario. The best moments of my married life have been spent on a sailboat in the waters of New England, the most relaxing moments alone in a tub trying to recreate the soothing impact of the hot soaking baths I so enjoyed in Japan. Without question, however, it is the Aegean that has most influenced my life over the last 50 years.

The Aegean has offered me a repository of riches historical, archaeological, cultural, aesthetic, and a treasure trove of personal experiences that have helped educate the adult me. My initial exposure to this particular body of water was the month my husband and I spent on the island of Crete celebrating our first anniversary to compensate for that disastrous honeymoon. Our good fortune began on the ferry from Piraeus where we made friends with a simpatico German couple who invited us to their cabin for breakfast and a shower after a night spent campedout on the deck with our sleeping pads and bags. Best of all, after discovering our very similar plans, they suggested we travel together in their Mercedes.

What we may have forfeited in adventure, we more than made up for in comfort and good company. What a wonderful month we had touring the ancient sites of Knossos and Phaistos, exploring the caves at Mattila, spending hours swimming in crystal blue waters, and enjoying leisurely Greek meals with fresh fish and seafood (the Greeks are insistent on the difference), a variety of tasty and hearty salads, hand-cut potatoes fried in olive oil, the best crunchy bread outside of France.

We drank a lot those evenings—ouzo, retsina, and countless bottles of Amstel beer. Our waiter calculated our bill by simply counting the empty plates and bottles littering the table. We loved exploring the little villages with their whitewashed houses, watching the fishermen mend their nets and the shepherds with their flocks of goat and sheep often blocking the roads. When the opportunity arose ten years later for me to spend a year teaching abroad with my family in tow, Greece was the obvious choice.

Courtesy of the Fulbright program, we spent 1980-81 and 1987-88 in Thessaloniki, the second-largest city of Greece located on the Thermaic Gulf. Almost every evening included a stroll along its shores, most weekends we camped in Sarti, Halkididi, home to some of the world's most beautiful beaches. We have returned to Thessaloniki and Sarti for a month most every summer and recently brought our daughters, son-in-law, and grandsons on what we came to call the Barstow family pilgrimage. We have also managed over the years to visit a dozen Aegean islands in the company of two Greek couples who have become our closest friends. And we've explored the Aegean coast of Turkey, or what the Greeks still call Asia Minor, home to some of the best-preserved Greek ruins, most especially Ephesus and Pergamon. We had the good fortune to visit this area years before the hordes of tourists began to arrive.

There's so much fascinating history surrounding the Aegean which we have enjoyed learning. The families of our Greek friends moved to Thessaloniki during the great 1923 population exchange in which over a million Turks and Greeks were relocated to majority Muslim or Christian areas. Many Greek families were resettled in parts of Halkidiki, each given several parcels of land including olive orchards and less fertile plots for their houses closer to the sea. Towns developed over time and some, including Sarti, were occupied by the Germans during the second world war. Despite the brutality of the occupation, many Halkidikians moved to Germany as guest workers when unable to earn a living at home. All that has now changed with throngs of European tourists flocking to Halkidiki led by the children of the Germans who learned of the region's beauty during the war and by the guest workers whose time abroad provided them with the language skills and financial resources to build hotels and restaurants catering to free-spending visitors.

When we first discovered Sarti in 1980, it seemed a bucolic and undeveloped region with more goats and sheep than people. We were soon well known throughout the village and often invited for ouzo and simple appetizers following our evening walk. One February weekend when the few "rooms for rent" facilities were all closed, a shepherd offered us a bed in his cottage, my first experience "camping" indoors without running water. As the tourists began to arrive in increasing numbers these past decades, this simple house has been replaced by a bar, our favorite family cove is overrun with beachgoers from all corners of Europe, ugly hotels dominate the landscape and the town has spread for several miles up and down the coast. We miss the village we had grown to love and despair at the problems that prosperity has introduced. Still, we understand why the villagers themselves, only two generations removed from displacement and poverty, embrace their new reality.

As for Thessaloniki, it too has a fascinating history. Prior to the population exchange and the world wars, it was one of the most diverse cities on the planet with Jews, Christians, and Muslims living and working in relative harmony. During the 500-year rule of the Ottomans, Jewish refugees from the Spanish Inquisition were welcomed to the city and were able to work freely beside Orthodox shopkeepers.

The Muslims were forced out during the population exchange as the Greek refugees flooded in from Asia Minor and the Nazis eventually deported and killed virtually the entire population of Jews. Throughout the 20th century, the city became more and more insistently "Greek" and the material artifacts of this history ultimately disappeared from view. Most mosques and synagogues were destroyed by a massive fire in 1917 without being rebuilt, and the city later destroyed Jewish and Muslim properties that might have distracted from the classical and Byzantine monuments deemed central to the city's nationalistic identity and cultural heritage.

The Thessaloniki we came to know is now fully Greek. We love exploring its classical ruins and Byzantine churches, we enjoy all aspects of its culture, but we also appreciate knowing this history and discovering traces of its legacy. We especially appreciate the Turkish influence on the cuisine of Northern Greece that is somehow fresher and tastier than the typical Athenian fare. Over the decades we have spent visiting Thessaloniki, the city has grown bigger and more modern. The Thermaic bay is no longer polluted, restaurants and bars have become more cosmopolitan; Thessaloniki is a major academic and business center, it is home to an international film festival, has a vibrant arts scene, and welcomes visitors from throughout the world. Very recently Thessaloniki has finally discovered the value of reclaiming its rich multicultural history. As it adds Muslim and Jewish sites to the marketing of the city, new sources of tourism and their dollars inevitably follow. This complicated and fraught history of northern Greece is, of course, a direct result of its location and the prominent role in world trade the Aegean Sea played in ancient and pre-modern times. The Chinese, by the way, are investing heavily in Greek ports with hopes of benefitting from a reinvigorated Aegean trade. Ironically, this is occurring at the same time thousands of desperate migrants continue to risk the Aegean's often treacherous waters in search of a better life in "the West."

Somehow all this weighty significance adds an ineffable element to our more personal relationship to the Aegean. We love how pleasant and easy it is to swim in this very salty sea. Buoyancy helps as does the welcoming temperature of the water. We love the openness of its beaches with no fences, no ticket booths, no obvious class divisions. Building is not allowed on beaches—there are no private homes, no hotels, no municipalities controlling access. Some restaurants have tables and chairs at the beach, some establishments rent boats, chairs, umbrellas, or serve drinks, but any permanent structure must be located across the road. How very different from the beaches of my youth. We have taken to observing sensible Greek beach schedules with morning swims between 10:00 a.m. and noon and early evening ones between 5:00 and 7:00 p.m. A light dinner usually follows a shower and a walk around 9:00 at night as we watch the moon rise above the sea.

There is so much more we appreciate about Greek culture, especially its positive attitude toward children and the joy surrounding food, whether at home or in a restaurant. Meals eaten out are always family-style with groups of six or more (one almost never sees a table for two) gathered around a table filled with a plethora of dishes: grilled anchovies, sautéed calamari, whole barbounia alongside tsatsiki, melitzana salata, the essential village salad of peppers, onions, cucumbers, tomatoes, olives and feta (lettuce is served separately), vegetable dishes of beans or beets or zucchini. Many restaurants have playgrounds and children seemingly run free with no one annoyed by their presence and all adults assuming responsibility for their safety. It is thanks to living in Greece that my daughters would rather eat salad than anything else. On the other hand, they both declared themselves vegetarians after seeing the lambs marked with red x's prior to slaughter for Easter. We have now enjoyed five Paschas (the Greek word for Easter is the etymon for Passover), a week-long celebration culminating in a truly sumptuous midnight feast though recently goat has replaced lamb as the central meat.

I suppose if I had not left Chicago as a young woman, if I still had good friends there, I might find myself returning to Lake Michigan more often. Certainly, Chicago is a city worth visiting and has its own colorful history and lively nightlife. The Aegean's significance for me personally is partly a matter of chance… we just happen to have a great deal in common with our close Greek friends who have shared so much of their history and culture with us. It may also be easier fully to appreciate another country and its waters when viewed from the outside. The grass may not be greener, but the sea is clearly bluer.

MOVING THE STATUE
Joe Taylor

I don't know if you ever heard of The Moving Statue in Cork? It happened in Ballinspittle, near Kinsale in 1985. A passer-by stopped to pray at a roadside statue of the Virgin Mary as she passed by in the evening, and she suddenly noticed that the statue was moving! As the word spread, people went there to see what it was all about. I was a first-year student in University College Cork at the time and the whole place was agog with it. The prevailing view at the college was that it was all a hoax and just a ruse to get tourism into Kinsale. That was my view too.

I had gone to secondary school with the Christian Brothers in the North Mon. in Cork. I liked science a lot, so I was not into the paranormal. The year I graduated from the Mon.; the Irish government introduced free university entrance for all students who passed the Leaving Cert. which is how I got into the college. I wouldn't have been able to go there otherwise as we didn't have the money for it. UCC was a great place then and still is! It was now full of a great diversity of students; unlike the way it was before free education.

The college is a lovely place. You can get there from the town walking up the Western Road through the gates and over a bridge, past a little river leading to the college itself with its beautiful buildings and gardens. It was a small college then and everyone milled around the Quad (as the main quadrangle was known) or went to the Men's Club. This club was not that at all but really just a large room with tables and chairs where you'd get coffee and pastries.

Nor was it for men only and a lot of the girls went in there too which was a change from ten years before that. I went in there one day on a break and seeing a table with students I knew, I went over and sat with them. There was one lovely girl there and I asked her view on the statue and if she thought it was a hoax. She said, "Time will tell, stranger things have happened." I asked her name and she said, "Mary Kate." I told her, "I'm Finbarr. I'm a first-year science student". She said, "So you're from the dark side! I'm studying arts and humanities." I said, "Well, Mary Kate, maybe one night we could go together to see the moving statue to make a determination on it from both the scientific and artistic sides."

I was immensely proud of myself then for skillfully introducing the idea of getting together without, as I thought, being too obvious. She saw right through that though, but laughed and said, "You're a wily one. I will have to keep my eye on you in the future."

"How about a drink at Starry's one night, or evening, what do you think?" I said.

"I'll have to think about that and ask around about you before I go out with you."

"Fair enough. You'll find out that I'm relatively straight forward and have no big sins on my conscience, at least that I know of. You know some of the people that I know, so you can check with them if you want to."

The next time I met her, I asked her again and she replied, "Well, there's no harm in it, I suppose."

Starry's is another institution near the college, just like the Men's Club. It's a decent size pub and lounge whose official name is The Western Star and is about a mile from the college outside the gates. It's on the Western Road next to the Greyhound Track and is also near Fitzgerald's Park and the Cricket Club on the Mardyke.

We met in the lounge there as we agreed on Saturday. She had a blouse and pants on and I was in corduroy pants and a light shirt. When the barman came around, she ordered a gin and tonic and I had a pint of Murphy's stout. I asked her what she was studying.

"I'm reading Hemmingway and James Joyce this term. The Joyce book is Dubliners. I'm sure you have heard of it. He writes of ordinary Dublin people and their inner lives and thoughts. It's a classic of western fiction. He must have listened very carefully to people going about their daily routines. Some of his characters live ordinary lives and others have addictions with friends trying to help them. I'm not that gone on Hemmingway though, he's full of piss and vinegar. All of his heroes are macho men, either going to war or looking for the next one. I don't think that the mark of a strong man is to be sticking spears in bulls and then cutting off their gonads. There's a different sort of courage that a lot of women and men have which is just to lead a good life and be decent. So, what sort of man are you and what are you studying?" she said.

"I'm a first-year in science, studying chemistry and physics. This week we had lab experiments in chemistry where I and a partner generated chlorine gas in an apparatus and used it in a chemical reaction. A second experiment was to demonstrate Boyle's Laws of Gases." She butted in then and said,

"That chlorine gas one sounds dangerous. Wasn't that stuff used in wars to kill soldiers?"

"You're right about that but we take a lot of precautions. The gas apparatus is in a sealed fume hood. Then we have goggles over our eyes when we are doing the work and we always wear fresh lab coats too." With that, she said, "Oh I'd like to see you in your scrubs, I'm sure you'd look like Dr. Kildare who used to be on the TV. My mam had a huge crush on him."

Other friends we knew came in then and ordered some drinks, so we got another round with them. As the night moved on, I asked Mary Kate if I could walk her home. She agreed, and we held hands together. When we came to her house it was a beautiful, detached house in Douglas. I asked her again if she was up for a jaunt down to Kinsale to see the statue. "It's the only way we'll know if this is true or a lark and it would be a good day out anyway," I said. She agreed to that and we agreed to meet at the bus station near the river in Cork City. We would get the two o'clock bus since I had a part-time job in the morning. With that, we parted but not before I kissed her on the lips, and she responded sweetly.

When Saturday came, I was at the bus station when Mary Kate arrived, and we jumped on the bus when it came along. We went upstairs and sat together. The bus was almost full, and it was a lovely day. I'd guess that some of the passengers were heading for the statue in the evening like us.

Kinsale itself is a huge sailing destination and is a beautiful place known all around the world. There are hundreds of boats in the inner and outer harbors ranging from dinghies to hundred feet long world mega yachts and anything else in between. In addition to that, Kinsale is also renowned for culinary excellence and the restaurants and hotels are legendary. With plenty of time to spare, we wandered around the town and looked at the bars and restaurants. The best one we found was The Spaniard. The wine and food there were excellent.

Later in the day, we went to get the bus to go out to the statue. When we got there a crowd had already gathered. It dawned on us: How we would get back to Cork plus we needed to get back to Kinsale first. Regardless, we took our chances when the next bus came and started our ride to the statue.

This bus was packed too, as it wended its way through the town and then headed out to Ballinspittle. It was a short ride, though, and we were soon there. When we got off the bus, we were still a half-mile away from the site and there were so many people there that it took a long time to get to the statue.

When we got there, it was a mighty sight with the crowds and the police and the statue itself. A cordon of ropes kept the viewers back twenty yards from the Grotto. On top of that, we were at the back of the crowd and we could hardly see anything. Then a large group of people left and we were able to go to the front and see the panorama before us. The statue was a life-size plaster image of Mary painted in blue and white in a small ravine in cliffs above the road. The words "I am the Immaculate Conception" were inscribed below it. The head of the statue was surrounded with small, white electric bulbs in the form of a halo. We were only about twenty yards away from it.

As twilight came, a calm came over the gathered throng as this was the expected hour of the apparition. Then, slowly, the statue began to flicker and appeared to shake gently. A lot of the crowd knelt silently then. Mary Kate and I did too. We stayed there for an hour, but not on our knees. We then began to think about getting home. This was a problem. We had burned our bridges a bit unless we could hitch a ride back to Cork. Otherwise, we would be stuck there for hours. As luck would have it, some college friends of ours were leaving too; so, we got a ride home with them. The car was an old Hillman van and there were already three others in it as well as the driver. So, we crouched in the back together. Of course, all the talk on the journey was about the statue. Was it real or just an optical illusion, brought on by the state of the nation and some mass hysteria? We mostly thought it was just a trick of the light but the driver, Mick, thought otherwise. He was a psychology fourth-year student. He said, "It's common to attribute things like this to delusions, but sometimes the phenomenon could be paranormal. So, I'll keep an open mind on this for a while and not be jumping to hasty conclusions". We continued to debate the pros and cons of the issue as we traveled the bumpy road back to Cork. But, to be truthful, Mary Kate and I were more interested in each other. The way back was tight but that was what we wanted, to be together and kissing and cuddling all the way home.

Back at the College the next Monday, we all gathered again at the Men's Club. The main topic of conversation was the long-forgotten rule that you could not cross the Quad unless you were a fourth-year student. The Quad is a rectangle of beautiful lawn about a hundred yards with two stone paths crossing it. In the previous week, the president of the college had decided to enforce this rule mainly because many of the new influx of students were not complying with it. I said,
"I like that tradition and was looking forward to exercising the privilege in time." Of course, the others mocked me for that. As for the statue, no one had any more comments.

Mary Kate and I went out to the statue a few times again. At the height of its fame, the statue attracted hundreds of thousands of people, some hoping for miracles. Two women claimed to have seen the statue sway gently. Others said they saw the statue's hands and feet move from side to side

The fame of the statue lasted over three years until one day the local newspaper, The Examiner, broke the news that the statue had been damaged. Apparently, a trio of Pentecostalists in their twenties from the North of Ireland had taken sledgehammers to the statue in the dark of night. They were arrested by the police a few hours later in Kinsale as they were making their way back up home. They had smashed the head, halo and hands of the statue with their hammers and a crowbar. During the attack, one of the few worshipers who were there shouted, "You must be Satan to do something like this" to which one of the vandals shouted back "You're worse to be worshipping false gods".

The vandals, shortly after, were jailed of course and the statue rebuilt and painted as before. Sadly, some of the mystical magic of the place seemed to pall then as if some of the spirit there had gone. Some said that it was the time of year while others thought that the Virgin herself had departed. In just a few years it was just an oddity and less and less people went out there.

Mary Kate and I continued to date for a while, but our own bond also seemed to weaken. Then I heard she was seeing another boy at the college and all the enchantment had gone. Our magical summer had come and gone, and our lovely time together was over.

Years later, when I returned to Cork on a trip to see family, I looked Mary Kate up too. She had married a merchant banker and had two lovely girls with him by then. She herself now worked in a bookstore in the town and I walked in there one day to say hello to her. She was the same lovely Mary Kate and we talked about the old days and said we would stay in touch.

We didn't, of course, but I wish I had. I regretted not pursuing her when I had the chance.

HOME/HOMELAND
Mel Jolly

From my childhood forward, I never really thought much about America being my homeland. Instead, I always seemed to have the impression I was here just temporarily; that the manner in which we as blacks were treated suggested we really were not wanted here; that we should go back to wherever it was we supposedly came from.

It wasn't until the late 1950s, during my high school years, that I saw any attempt to challenge the status quo. The south had had its way for years, but at last, both black and white college students decided enough hatred had been spread over too many lifetimes. It is to those courageous humans that I raise my glass in a salute toward their resolve to make our heterogeneous country feel more like home for all.

Think back upon times when you wanted to do something, but everyone told you it would be best if you just left things alone and didn't "rock the boat." I can recall two instances when I was put in that potential position. The first was during my elementary school years: My uncle was a quasi-musician, but he allowed me to take his prized clarinet to school. When I proudly took his treasured instrument to the music classroom, the teacher almost immediately asked me when and how I obtained the clarinet. I don't know whether or not my answer satisfied him. However, I do remember he ignored me for the entire class period. I was given no attention, not even a glance in my direction; it was very clear I was not wanted there. So much for my musical pursuits!

The second instance in which I was put in the position of "don't rock the boat" occurred years later when I was a high school student and a well-known basketball player on the high school team. I decided to diversify my interests in sports, so I borrowed an old wooden tennis racket and went to tennis practice. The tennis coach knew who I was and saw me approach the courts, only as I looked toward him, he looked away. Again, I was ignored in my attempt to do something different. I continued to stand on the sidelines hoping for some instruction or guidance, but none came, and I eventually left. In reality, the coach won our stand-off, because I didn't "rock the boat."

With the onset of the Civil Rights Movement, not "rocking the boat" evolved into a struggle to push forward beliefs of equality, beliefs of equal treatment of soldiers who fought and died for a country that had not always been welcoming, beliefs that "go back home" signs should be removed from front yards. It saddens me to think that American citizens are once again being asked to choose sides. On the other hand, seeing the theatrical production *Hamilton* inspired me: I was encouraged by what transpired on that stage.

I thought a black man being elected President of the United States was a monumental achievement. Perhaps even that pales though, in comparison to the roles so many ethnicities and non-stereotypical Broadway actors portrayed in *Hamilton*. As I left the theatre, it was impossible not to think that this is what America truly should be like – a place for everyone to sit at the same table and to not only have a conversation, but also develop an understanding that in reality, we all want the same thing: the chance, or equal opportunity, to serve our homeland and to make it a better place in which to live. Surely that is not asking too much!

HOMELAND AND HERITAGE
Phoebe Huang

For most of my life, I assumed China was my homeland - by birthright. I can name Kunming as my birthplace; I believe my bloodline to be 100% Han Chinese. But I now understand this was only an invention, a fiction in my mind. Reality hit when the Chinese Consulate in New York denied me a visa to "go home." I was denied because neither the diplomatic passport that brought me to America nor my U.S. naturalization papers could prove my Chinese name was my Chinese name.

How long has "Homeland" been a fluid notion? Ask the Muslims who inhabited India for generations to name their homeland after being kicked out and made to resettle in what became Pakistan. Ask the people who were born in Germany to Turkish emigres, to name their homeland. Here you will find that "blood Germans" do not consider these citizens part of the Vaterland. Yet Turkey does not appear to be their homeland either.

For me, everything is up in the air if China is no longer my homeland.

Does it matter?

Whereas the word "home" is packed with some of life's most soulful emotions: belonging, a place where one is forever welcome, a place to rest one's head, "homeland" adds a layer of gravitas - one's roots, one's cultural tradition, one's ultimate ties.

In his *Collected Essays*, James Baldwin notes: "These people (Europeans) cannot be, from the point of view of power, strangers anywhere in the world; they have made the modern world, in effect, even if they do not know it. The most illiterate among them are related, in a way that I am not, to: Dante, Shakespeare, Michelangelo, Aeschylus, Da Vinci, Rembrandt, and Racine. Out of their hymns and dances come Beethoven and Bach. Go back a few centuries and they are in their full glory - but I am in Africa watching the conquerors arrive."

So even while blacks invented jazz, the blues, early rock 'n roll, and dominate sports, maybe these achievements lacked sufficient longevity or gravitas to suit Baldwin: They didn't, at his moment in time, stand up to Mozart and Michelangelo. He also suggests that America is not his homeland.

To put this in context, we are, after all, tiny grains of sand in the universe. "The human race is just a chemical scum on a moderate-sized planet," according to Steven Hawking. Or, Carl Sagan put the point vividly in 1994 when discussing the famous "Pale Blue Dot" photograph taken by Voyager I. "Our planet," he said, "is nothing more than 'a mote of dust suspended in a sunbeam'."

To feel more substantial, maybe we need cloaks of legitimacy.

Is this what a "homeland" replete with cultural traditions does for us, provide legitimacy? Is this desire for validation why I had pride in calling China my homeland, have basked in the reflected glory of Chinese achievements, even though I had nothing to do with the invention of porcelain, the compass, or gunpowder, nor has anyone in my family. Yet I am Chinese by birthplace and blood, and these are Chinese contributions to the world. Isn't this also why people everywhere cling to their family's accomplishments, their lineage?

Only in my case, I think the affiliation was most influenced by my parents: They were proud to be Chinese, respectful of their origins. I think by osmosis, I became prideful too.

Still, it has been a zigzag assimilation. My third and fourth-grade teacher, Mrs. Brogan, was fond of declaring to the class that Chinese people were so polite. Whether or not she had direct experience of this, I was the only Chinese student in the class, in the school. Those pronouncements did not fill me with pride, only caused me to squirm in my seat with embarrassment.

At that time, I did not know of Japan's ravaging of China during WWII, nor did I know of China's humiliation when divided into Spheres of Influence at the hands of Western Powers, a time when posted signs read: "No Chinese and dogs allowed" at the entrance to public parks in Shanghai.

So, my pride in birthright was, to a degree, inherited, the way I inherited my parents' genes.

Had James Baldwin's parents been proud to be black, to have come from Africa, would he have written the lines: "but I am in Africa watching the conquerors arrive."

And what if my father had not been educated in the scope and sweep of Chinese civilization, but knew only that he, along with dogs, was prohibited from entering his city's parks, would he have been so prideful? Surely not. Nor would I have been, with that alternate inheritance.

In grade school, a handful of us were picked to create the scenery for a school play. We had sheets of paper so large a few of us could kneel on them to finish the painting. Eddie Stevens, the class-wise guy, and therefore the most popular boy, squatted next to me and asked why, if I could not return to Red China, I didn't just go back to Green China? Instead of a slow dissolve, I was able to laugh at his teasing.

Now, sixty years after grade school, fifty years after becoming a naturalized US citizen, I revisit what relevance my long-held beliefs have or have not.

My children, born in this country, have no ambivalence whatsoever. They view China as part of my history, but not so relevant to their lives. Their feet are solidly planted in American soil: there is no question that they will be rooting for the American team in any international women's volleyball competition, not the Chinese women.

My position is less clear, even though I feel allegiance to the United States, even though China no longer views me as one of theirs.

One explanation, I believe, is that I am a first-generation immigrant: I have experienced assimilation while my children have not. I still remember sitting at the back of my kindergarten classroom - in tears for days? weeks? while words I could not understand swirled around me. No one was unkind. Only, I was alien.

My parents, fluent in English, spoke only English to my brother and me at home, to give us a boost. Still, that separateness lingered, though it was measurably softened by a note I was slipped in second grade. I opened the scrap of paper to read, "You are cute. Kenny Kramer." Wherever Kenny is now, he has my thanks. His was my first real welcome.

Adding to my ambivalence is the wavering sentiment of Americans towards 'foreigners,' read that "anyone who looks different." Esi Edugyan, a Canadian author whose family emigrated from Ghana, was asked if she believed we live in a color-blind society, a society where race goes unnoticed. In her book, *Dreaming of Elsewhere*, she observed, "I confess I find the notion ridiculous. We are as we ever were, inclined to quick judgments based on what we see. And all too often what we see are the differences."

I believe she is stating fact, not being unduly critical. I am aware of biases in my own behavior, ridiculous as that is, and chide myself. Maybe this is part of being human.

The precariousness for "foreigners" is heightened when the Leader in Chief, Ruler of the Free World, rails against this and that visibly different ethnic group; the latest against Chinese.

My worry is that he and others could whip up negative sentiment to a kind of frenzy that makes living in this country uncomfortable. Consider how Japanese citizens were interned during World War II. Less well known is that 11,507 people of German ancestry were interned during the war, comprising 36.1% of the total internments under the US Justice Department's Enemy Alien Control Program. So being a naturalized citizen in this country does not carry unequivocal acceptance.

"Homeland," in the past, signified one's ethnic, blood, cultural ties to a piece of geography, a landmass which you inalienably belonged to, a land mass you could not be ejected from precisely because of these ethnic, blood ties, and cultural roots.

All seems to have changed. Globalization, political shifts, terrorism, famine, endless migration are altering who can call any piece of geography their "homeland." Plus, it seems, almost anyone can be ejected from anywhere.

Alongside me, scores of Russians, Poles, Turks, Czechs, Cubans, Indians, Ethiopians, Rwandans, Syrians, Palestinians, to name just a few groups, have all lost their original homelands.

The United States is on a trajectory that will render Caucasian whites a minority. At that point, whose homeland will this country be?

Maybe we're approaching a point where "homeland" can best be defined by one's contribution. Just as one cannot call a place "home" if one has not contributed to it in some way by investments of psychic energy, labor, capital, and caring; and, better still, by improvements, maybe one can call a defined geography one's homeland only by making similar investments.

I like this definition of "homeland." It leaves behind vague nostalgia, the notion of birthright. It suggests one has to earn a homeland. It loses the entire idea of entitlement. Just as I had no hand in developing gunpowder, I have no current standing in China: I have made no contribution there. My efforts will continue to be here.

I'm still working out how I feel about heritage.

LOSS

The doctor gave her grim news
She wept silently without tears
Cold hungry and alone

Vaillancourt

The warmth of your hands
Your tender breath on my nape
I am imprinted

Danese

Worry thrives at times
Gnaws, rises like Easter bread
Then diminishes.

Ursillo

LEAVING
Bernard "Bing" Bartick

One never leaves anything
Everything stays with us
Those we love
Those who aggravate us
Beautiful places
Ugly places
Places we have lived
Places we have dreamed of living
Places we have gone
Places that we have left
Places that we wished we had been
We move forward because we have no choice
We stay behind because we want to
We are embedded in our life
Our dreams
What happened?
What was?
What we wished could have been
It is all we
We move on
We do not leave
Everyone and everything remains in our minds, hearts, and souls

THE PHILOSOPHER
Andy Rosenzweig

The detective smiles a little, just before a bullet explodes into his left eye, shattering it, driving its way past destroyed tissue and tiny fountains of blood to the medulla oblongata, the part of the brain that controls breathing.

He doesn't suffer long is what the coroner, later on, tells the thirty-year-old wife. The new widow is wearing a tan summer dress and dark brown heels. Her ash blond hair is worn short. Through barely controllable sobs, streaked makeup, she asks the coroner if she should tell that to their two little children.

How do you tell your mother that she's raised a sociopath? That's how Willy Naulls thinks of himself lately, when he thinks of all the things, he's been a part of, how he sometimes lets himself get into situations that pour misery into other people's lives, like the latest one…by far the worst he's done. And when he thinks about it, he's still not sure if he got led or he was doing the leading.

A warm, muggy city night, black shimmering asphalt and drab gray concrete collects heat and leaks it back into the air. Three young men sit on the brown cement stoop of a dark red brick building, one of a thousand spread over hundreds of city blocks. They're dressed alike, in loose fitting sweat-shorts, colorful mesh basketball jerseys, high tops with no socks, gold chains.

"We gotta make a score."

The oldest one ignores the remark, answers with a non-sequitur:

"Look around man. Broken bricks, cinder blocks, hubcaps, shopping carts, bags of garbage, shit collecting in vacant lots… makes this place almost uninhabitable. It's a sign."

"Sign of what?"

"Deterioration of civilization…I tell you we becoming uncivilized."

Willie Naulls, Plato to his friends, IQ over one hundred and thirty, easily aces every subject in high school, barely opening a book. He's been admitted to five colleges.

"Where you want to go, Willie?"

"M.I.T., I guess."

He thinks about the last time he was home, sitting in the tiny kitchen, looking at large pieces of peeling yellowish paint on the walls. The gray speckled linoleum is cracked and uneven.

"I'm gonna have to get a third job," his mother says.

"Counselor said don't worry bout the money, momma, once you admitted, they find ways to get you financing...combination of scholarships, loans."

"Who gonna buy you some nice clothes, pay for your carfare home on weekends? Maybe the dean...or the college president?"

Sometimes he sits on the tarpaper rooftop of his building gazing at the city lights and the distant glow and flickering of stars and thinks about his circumstances. Half the time thinking college just is not in the cards.

Still, by sixteen he's read everything by James Baldwin - novels, memoirs, short stories. He thinks every bit of his writing, even the fiction, is memoir. After all, he says to himself, the little fucker didn't pluck this shit out of the air.

Willie's father died in South Carolina, in a juke joint, little more than an oversized one-room shack made of graying clapboard, off a country road, in a dispute over a woman he'd just met. His mother never says much more than "your father didn't know enough to stay away from trouble...would always be in the wrong place...finally was at the wrong time." He was shot and killed by an off-duty deputy sheriff he'd been arguing with. Willie's father was unarmed.

Cops up here are only slightly better than southern sheriffs, he thinks. He's been stopped and searched so many times that it's almost as routine as eating out once a week with his Moms, who has always worked two jobs.

"Cops waste their time stopping me and my boys...real gang-bangers laughing their asses off at the pigs."

"Watch your mouth."

"Sorry momma."

"You answer that letter?"

"What letter?"

Wait-listed for M.I.T. Every time they discuss college she talks about the importance of an education. She never even made it to high school. She knows though, she knows.

"White man never going to accept a nigger like me. No amount of preaching, education, integration, affirmative action, diversity training, inclusion, what have you; none of that bullshit going to erase the fact that I'm a dark man in a white man's world...and the white man is insecure...only going to let us go so far, throw us a bone here or there, make us think we moving ahead...Sheet...we treading water, momma, that's all. How many times I got to be stopped, searched, treated like less than a man, like I'm some kind of sub-human mother? I'm a walking, talking self-fulfilling prophecy. They treat me like an anti-social unproductive close to worthless lower-class mo-fo...how you think I'm gonna behave?"

She stares at him, stuffs a Virginia Slim into her lips, bends over the stove at one of the jets until the tip of the cigarette is aflame. Her faded red housedress, gray geometric designs, stretches as if it might rip. She straightens up, pulls hard, smoke bursting from her mouth and nose.

"You being defeatist Willie, becoming your own worst enemy."

Tuesday night Willy and his boys follow the waiter from the Italian restaurant on 115th and Pleasant Avenue to a project built in the sixties, thirteen red brick towers of decay, as if the maintenance department has been on strike for fifty years. Carver Houses, between Madison and Park, from 99th to 106th Street - close to three thousand people crammed into a community designed for half that, people who have little choice about where they get to live, working mediocre jobs, navigating the surrounding streets and the paths and buildings of the projects.

The waiter stops at a bench about a block from his house, sits with a man he knows, and a younger woman about forty, dressed in a thin white blouse and blue cut-offs. They offer him a drag. He inhales deeply, sits looking up through the canopy of an old maple tree. A few minutes later he thanks them, continuing his walk home.

A night later they follow the same routine. Willie tells them it's time. The waiter's about ten feet ahead of them, then five, then they're on him. There's a short scream and a flurry of arms and fists swinging, feet kicking, all aimed at the waiter. Hard to imagine how his bones aren't shattered. People stand around watching, but no one says anything. Blows rain down from every direction. He's on his hands and knees, moaning. Knuckles pound his face, blood seeps on to his white shirt, hands going through his pockets, accompanied by a few laughs.

Later, in the police station, he says he can't recall the words they said. The cops show pictures, ask him what they looked like.

"Black, man, three of them," he says.

The waiter's black, too, but light skinned. He's from Cuba, came across in 1980 on the Mariel boatlift. Castro released a bunch of career criminals and psychos and sent them in a flotilla that lasted months, ninety miles to Miami. He wasn't one of those. He was a waiter in Havana and knew he'd find work in America. He had a skill, could earn a living anywhere. He crowded onto a rickety craft and minded his own business. He still has a thick accent.

Then he remembers something - the tall guy slapped one of the others when he used a name – "Plato, let's book man, the cops will be here soon," is what he said.

"Could you recognize them?"

"I don't know. Show me some more pictures."

A hundred and thirty-eight dollars split three ways, almost fifty each. They're in the last booth in a seedy bar near the Tri-Boro Bridge, minutes from where they live. Everyone in the place thinks they're bad news.

Plato is six-three, with chiseled muscles, a wide nose that covers half his face, and full lips. He wears a light green V-neck sweater over a white tee.

"Spoils of war, know what I'm saying?"

They stare at him, stupid expressions on their faces. They're often taken for brothers, each with full lips, broad noses, and cornrows.

"To the victor go the spoils…you all never heard that shit?"

He sits up straight when the two detectives walk into the bar - two paddy-looking sons of bitches…walk up the bar like they don't give a shit. The detectives look around, stop and focus on their booth, drill them with hard stares. One of them is older, a fat guy. The other looks about thirty.

"You three, hands on the table."

Stupid mothers… if we did have something, they'd be dead honky mothers, he thinks. The blinking red neon sign, Big Paul's, hangs over the shiny red enamel door of the one-story old brick building, between two plate glass windows. They're outside now spread eagled against the bricks. The window of the unmarked police cruiser is down.

"Him. The big one called Plato…that's him."

"Hey, Plato."

He turns to look at the younger detective, knows he's toast.

The waiter, still in the cruiser, puts his nose up to the rear window. The young detective slides back into the front passenger seat. "You sure it's them?"

"Yes. How'd you find them?" he says.

"Nickname file…how many Platos, you think we have in the city?"

Seconds later the detective is back out of the cruiser.

"You all is just doing your jobs, we unnerstan that…you all is the last line of defense, you know what I'm sayin?" Plato says.

Both detectives seem disgusted. The heavy one looks ready for retirement. He removes a cigarette from a pack in his left shirt pocket, takes it between his lips, and reaches into his trouser pocket for his lighter.

The younger one is all business, by the number's kind of guy, has the three still leaning against the bricks, feet wide apart, slowly and methodically patting them down.

"Turn and face the car!"

His rotund partner barely keeps his eyes on what's happening. Then the explosion and milliseconds pass, but it seems like an hour, everything in slow motion.

"Throw the gun from the car!"

The waiter tosses it onto the sidewalk, the sound of metal hitting concrete, making a dull sound. The fat detective drags him out and handcuffs him. Other police, lights blazing, sirens screaming, come on the scene, find the young detective on his back, on the sidewalk between the curb and the red brick wall of the bar, shirt soaked in blood. Mixed in are his partner's tears.

The waiter is arraigned the next day, a few weeks later pleads to manslaughter (tells the judge he's very sorry, he was aiming for the muggers.)

"Mo-fo was out for vigilante justice. Ain't right, you know what I'm saying – don't judge a man until you walked a mile in his shoes."

Willy Naulls thinks to himself - sociopath! I'm no better than any other remorseless mo-fo. Detective's dead, little kids never going to know their daddy (like me, he thinks.) Whole thing's totally fucked up. He read about the family in the Daily News. Wife's picture in the paper looked like she ain't stopped crying since it happened. In court, the judge told the waiter he was looking at life. Now he's good as done, Willy thinks. Fucked up, man. Fucked up. He's been thinking a stream of consciousness for days.

Later, in the booth in Big Paul's, they're sipping Bailey's Irish. The brown wood table is scarred with burns of fallen cigarettes. They stare across the booth at each other, silent, until the one closer to the wall finally says something.

"Plato, shut the fuck up man…I'm tired of your bullshit."

He takes a piece of paper from his pants, unfolds it, slides a red Bic lighter off the table, flicks the flint with his thumb a few times, until the tiny flame appears, sets the acceptance letter afire and drops it into the glass ashtray.

"What the fuck you doing, Plato?"

The burly owner/bartender comes around the bar, towering over them at the booth. He grabs the contents of a glass, pours it over the ashtray, extinguishing the flame. A slight hiss is barely heard over the loud guffaws of his friends. Acrid odor of moistened burnt paper envelops the small booth.

"I told you meatballs to behave yourselves you want to drink in here. What in God's name you think you're doing?"

"Doing nothing, Paul…"

ETERNAL UNHOLY WATER
Peggy Conti

I come to your fountain in sifting form
waxy eyed with arrowheads hidden
in pursuit of unbroken youth

have I drunk from this fount before?
is it the same unpurified formula bestowed?
on young in less sanctioned countries

of swindlers offering great minds for sale
if only you drink the moneychangers' liquid

Here drink…
You must thirst

or might it be the same unholy water
drunk at Lourdes where the wounded
of mind and body cast aside crutches

so, they may walk upright
only to crawl halfway home…

*Nestled here in scabbed palms,
sprung from seepage of blemished water

are corrosive lies and brittle
covenants handed back from crimes
committed all those many years ago

how will I trust you with my prudence?

if I am erased who
will fight to part
good water from bad

will the allotment be equal?

will I then have a balance of memory to tell
the children what really happened here

~~~

*Nestle Company
In 1977, Nestle Company was accused of deceitful marketing practices against women in impoverished countries falsely promoting the benefits of Nestle formula over breast milk. As a result of this unmitigated greed, a staggering number of babies died.

AN INACTIVE ACTIVIST

Peggy Conti

My Dad was a blue-collar union guy who did road construction. My mother a fiery immigrant who organized the factory she worked in during WWII. "There should be better quality control here. These wires are for the Boeings. Your uncle is a gunner on one of those planes. I want him home in the same condition as when he left to fight for Uncle Sam," she would say.

I remember my father picking me up from school in the Bumblebee, a '55 coupe. "She wasn't much to look at, so I painted her with a six-inch brush, lemon yellow, black bottom," said my father. He was an Army sergeant just back from the war. "Just got hired at the union plant downtown. Guess how much an hour?"

The men were tough. They got their muscles from hard labor. Not from pumping iron at some tony gym. The women could make a mean loaf of bread for supper and still carry an artful picket sign. "Whatever you do during the day, do it in solidarity. You will awake with a clean face in the morning," my mother's words. "Eat bread and onions before you steal a dime from some poor slob," my father's words.

And there you have it. My parents were not educated but with wisdom and humility, fought against injustices. Leaving a legacy of stop squawking, recognize a wrongdoing, and move. I think I have done that. I was a labor and community organizer in the 70s, 80s, and 90s against companies whose greed caused civil unrest, murder, and everlasting poverty. My fervent wish is I never achieve contentment. It immobilizes me. Anger is my only motivation. Now! If you will excuse me, I have an itch to move.

KATE
Deb Vaillancourt

Like a butterfly within me, I remember feeling that first little flutter and the gentle tapping and soft movement coming from my abdomen. A short time after that, a small hardness formed, and I felt great tenderness in the bonding that was happening so early on.

When I was in my 35th week, I visited the doctor's office for the beginning of a series of weekly office visits; this time with the partner obstetrician on staff. It was at the precise moment when I met this new physician that all my worst fears were realized. You see I knew. I always knew there was something wrong. The doctor took one look at me and said, "How many weeks did you say you were?" He immediately referred me to St. Margaret's Hospital in Dorchester, MA due to its state-of-the-art Neo-Natal Intensive Care Unit. It was 1980 and I was 32 years old.

I was induced for labor and told to lie on my left side. As I watched the Pitocin drip into my body, I started to feel very slight contractions. It didn't take long for the doctor to determine that my baby could not tolerate a normal delivery. The Pitocin was stopped.

The operating room was unusually cold. All around were silent, unfamiliar machines. At the foot of the narrow, aluminum bed laid coils of tubing to be used for some purpose unknown to me. I was instructed by a masked woman in green to lie still. Another masked woman entered, and the two women methodically counted and checked the many, shiny instruments that lay in formation to my left. I stared up and into two large saucer-like lights that now were unlit.

I felt them tugging at me as they pulled my baby's small, fragile body out of me. In place of a cry, I heard the sound of something rolling over near to me - an incubator. The words from the doctor when he first laid eyes on her had not shocked me. "She's sooo small!"

I was wheeled into a room on the maternity floor. I felt drugged and numb. Where was I? I wanted to just sleep; sleep to escape the nightmare that was happening in wakefulness. A heavy-set nurse with a stern look on her face came into my room and turned on the bright fluorescent light over my head. "I am here to take you to see your daughter. She is not doing very well." I was catapulted back into the nightmare.

The nurse helped me into a wheelchair. I began to cry, softly. With a light thud, the nurse dropped a box of tissues into my lap. She proceeded to wheel me down several, long, shiny-floored corridors to an elevator that resembled a freight elevator. When we got off the elevator, the nurse turned right and steered me down another corridor. It seemed late. There was no one around. Why were we in a basement? I could hear the nurse's heavy breathing. Where was she taking me? I was pushed through a glass double door which read "Neonatal Intensive Care Unit-Do Not Enter." Like a relay, I was transferred to another nurse. The new nurse was younger and seemingly kinder. She had dark brown eyes and wisps of dark shiny hair that poked out from the surgical cap she wore on her head. She was masked and covered from head to toe with protective clothing. She spoke gently to me.

"Hi. I am going to have to ask you to wash your hands. I have a mask for you to put on. Just take your time. I'm sorry to make you have to go through this but I'm sure you understand."
"I understand," I said. Did I?

Large, blue machines, a tangle of wires, beeping, lights, and open, glass incubators with the tiniest babies I had ever seen were everywhere I looked. Where was she? Where were they keeping my fragile butterfly? What would she look like?

I was wheeled straight, left and then to the right. I kept my head partially lowered. I was afraid of all of it; afraid for all the babies and for my own as they lay in the balance like a simulated baby purgatory.

She stopped my wheelchair alongside a large incubator with an elevated mattress. A tiny, grayish-blue body lay lifeless in front of me attached to too many tubes. She was tinier than I had imagined weighing in at 1 lb. 15oz. She had a small fuzz of reddish hair and she looked like she would fit in the palm of my hand. I knew, at that moment, that she would not live. I was encouraged to touch her but at first, I was afraid to for fear that she would jump and that the needles and wires would hurt her wee limbs. I did reach over and carefully, so carefully, stroked her little fuzzed head; my poor sick butterfly. I put my index finger into my baby's diminutive hand. She responded by wrapping her tiny fingers around my finger as any baby would do. A gift.

The next morning, I dialed the phone...slowly; each turn of the dial bringing me closer to the cruel truth. Would she have died during the night? The voice of the intensive care unit nurse could barely be heard amidst the background noise of whirring machines and endless beeps. Kate had survived the night.

That afternoon, the head pediatrician came up to my room and informed me that he recommended turning off the respirator as she was doing so poorly. She died just two short days after her birth. Testing done at a later date, revealed that my placenta broke down at about 24 weeks failing to provide Kate with the necessary nourishment to keep her properly fed. When my milk came in that evening, there was no one to feed.

JANIS
Bernard "Bing" Bartick

Bullied in high school
Voted "Ugliest Man on Campus" in college
The pain scarred your soul
You painted that soul with musical notes
This gave you temporary reprieve
All you wanted was to be loved
That love was found in music
But all songs have to end
As did your happiness when the show was over
Music masked the pain
Relief could not be found in fame
What now?
Drugs, alcohol, and death
The sound of silence
You were beautiful
Heaven always knew that
And now, so do we

WATER
Christina Danese

Is it too easy or sophomoric to be writing about the tears that come either soundlessly or with a body-wreaking force that drives me to my knees? Or the showers I take in a vain attempt to cleanse away the suffering or to regain some semblance of purpose and routine?

"Think of grief like a wave," I am counseled and am told that my choice is to dive through it or be crushed by it. What does it mean if I choose instead to tread or to float? I can derive no more meaning from any of this than I can of your being gone.

If you were here, you would wrap me in your love, kiss the salt from my eyes and make the world make sense again. But you are not here. There is only the void left by your undeniable presence into which I am pouring my heart and that, once filled, I must learn to swim across.

It helps that I am stubborn and strong, that in my best moments I am able to acknowledge and be grateful for the gift of having been loved absolutely.

I walk down to the beach with the dog where she can run off leash and I can search for myself (and for you) in the ocean. My days are a reflection of the water; they shift between brutal, spuming, white-capped, steel-colored rollers and crystalline placidity.

That you are gone, and I remain are facts as absolute as waves, powerless to the pull of gravity, are fated forever to advance upon and retreat from the shore.

EYES ONLY
Wendy Bradford

I parked the car. Now stopped, I masked myself, preparing to enter the store. Sighing my last free breath and spying my face quickly in the rear-view mirror,. I could see that the hairdo had lost its shape and needed the expert touch of my hairdresser. I traced the lines on my forehead, and they felt deeper or was that my imagination? It seemed strange to have grown older during this pandemic, of so little action and much self-isolation, where time has somehow melted unto itself.

Not normally a mirror gazer, at that moment I deliberately studied what I saw as objectively as I could. More wrinkles sprinkled around the eyes and above the crown of the nose. The eyes were as blue as usual, despite the glasses, they radiated several shades of blue, dark, and light. For a moment, they reflected the surrounding colors as a swimming pool does with the clouds, sun, and trees above it. As the bright sun blasted itself over the dashboard, the eyes took an eerie lightness. I was amazed and disturbed at the same time. Oh well, time to go.

As I walked into the grocery store, I wondered how people would really see me. More time was required to analyze a person when half of their face disappeared behind a mask. You could not see their smile. What were their intentions? What were yours?

Would they recognize the empathy in the windows of my mind and soul just with the widening creases of my eyes? Would they recognize a hidden smile? Maybe I needed just to remember to verbalize that smile. "Thank you for your help. Have a really nice day."

BEN (A.K.A. DAD)
Bernard "Bing" Bartick

My father, Ben, died when I was sixteen. He was my best friend. We actually have the same name, Bernard Benjamin Bartick. My mother did not want to call me Bernie, so she called me Bing after Bing Crosby and because of my overactive behavior where everything associated with me went bing, bang, bong. But that is another story. Ironically, we call our son, also with the same legal name, Bernie, and we like that name.

My father became very sick when he was fifty-three. He had heart disease, complicated by diabetes. He was bed-ridden for two years. During that time, I would sit with him for hour after hour talking about history and life. He had been a teacher, among other things. While he was sick, he wrote two books that were never published, one of which has disappeared.

My dad did not have a great life. He came from an Irish-German family with strong religious beliefs. He chose or was chosen to become a priest. The family was happy because back then it was believed that if you had a priest in the family, all would go to heaven. Just before his final vows, he decided the priesthood was not for him. His family was not happy with his decision. He was not disowned or ostracized, but he knew his family resented his decision enormously. This hurt him deeply. Then a telegram came to the house, with that dreadful phrase, "we regret to inform you." His brother, best man and best friend, had died of Malaria during World War II. He was devastated. He never fully recovered.

My mom and dad had four children. I was the third child. They say the third child is often a rebel and I fully fit that description. My target was my mother. I felt controlled. She was doing the best she could. There were economic worries and my father was never very healthy. My mother and I argued constantly. I fled to the safety of my father. He and my mother had issues, but he never said a bad word about her. He knew that life was asking of her way too much.

My father never said a cross word to me in his life. Even when he told me he would kick me in the ass if I did not make a success of myself. It was said in a kind, loving, and positive way. Besides he could not lift up either of his legs due to his illness. This belief in me led me to persevere even though I struggled in school due to my inability to sit still. Today they would call it ADHD. Then, there were no meds.

My siblings excelled in school. I did not. Today, two of them have Ph.D.'s. Yet I was the first to get a college degree and a master's degree. My Dad never compared me to anyone else. He inspired in me that I could and would achieve whatever I desired.

I was working in a sweat shop in the summer of 1961. The temperature was ninety-five degrees. The humidity was wetter than rain. At 3:00 p.m., my boss who did nothing, but said everything, came up to me and said, "has your father been sick? Your mother is picking you up shortly." Nothing else was said to me.

My Mother picked me up in our old red Pontiac. She said that when she came home from teaching summer school, she found my dad delirious. She immediately called our doctor who came right over. Dr. Force and said that my dad needed to go immediately to Laurence and Memorial Hospital by ambulance. Mom said that we were heading straight to the hospital.

When we entered the hospital room, my dad was in an oxygen tent and breathing poorly. His complexion was grey. My stomach turned inside out, but I said nothing.

My mother sent my brother and I home to make the necessary phone calls. We walked three miles each way making one stop at Saint Joseph's Church to pray.

Ed and I were back in the hospital room at 6:00 p.m. My Mom was just sitting there and staring into space. I looked at my dad in the oxygen tent. He was not breathing. Neither was I at that moment.

When I focused after a short while, there was a doctor in the room. He said to my Mother, "you know your husband was very sick?" Her answer was, he is dead, isn't he?" The doctor nodded his head and my stomach knotted.

Though the third child, I made most of the funeral arrangements. It was I who had my arm around my mother while the rosary was said at the wake as my mother cried silently. I never cried.

I never cried, that is, until I got home after the mass and burial. Then I went into the bathroom and sat on the toilet as if it were a chair and cried and cried and cried,

I had just lost my hero, mentor, and father. However, the loss was just physical. He lives on spiritually in my heart, mind, and soul. I think about him every day. Many times, when no one is looking, I find myself talking with him, especially when I am walking the beach.

Hello Dad! Goodbye Dad! See you soon!

OCTOMOM FOR MOTHER'S DAY
Cynthia F. Davidson

I am not one of her fourteen children
though we do belong to the same
human family. As Mother's Day
approaches I see Nadya Suleman
as another mother, not quite like me.
Famous for her octuplets, she carried
eight children safely in the same pregnancy
twelve years ago at age thirty-three
aided by the miracles of science and
in vitro fertilization. By then Nadya was
divorced after a four-year marriage in the '90s.
Already an IVF mom, she was raising one
set of twins, four sons and two daughters on her own.
In need of money she danced for men
in the California clubs despite her college degree.
The only child of an immigrant and
an Iraqi War veteran, what Nadya wanted
most was a family, without the hassles
of another husband, or compromising
her celibacy. She convinced Denis
to donate the sperm and Doctor Kamrava
did the deed in his petri dish. Agreeing to
implant all her eggs at once, instead of
dissuading the single mother of six,
cost him his medical license and plenty
of notoriety. Octomom Nadya was left
to face the music while he hid his assets
in an offshore island tax haven.
She's a bonafide American celebrity,
with multiple TV deals and her own
Wikipedia page, enduring the
hatred, stalkers, and death threats.
Fame doesn't always cover the bills.
Desperate to save her family from eviction
in 2012 she made a porno film for $8,000

Octomom Home Alone.
Why didn't Nadya sell her embryonic female
fruit? Extracted eggs are worth more than that
and she could have avoided all the rest
but it would have cost her the harvest.
Noah, Maliyah, Isaiah, Nariyah,
Jonah, Makai, Josiah, Jeremi

IT'S FINE
Dyann Boudreau

Over the course of five winters, I lost every member of my immediate family. It's okay, its fine, death is inevitable. I'm over the shock and confusion of their passing but I can't help feeling a bit peeved by the suddenness of it. I can almost convince myself that the four of them concocted some foolish prank to pack up and fly off, leaving me behind.

It's okay, it's fine when you lose your parents later in life. By then, your safety and security are not at risk. The worst of it is losing the people who care. The ones who jump up to put the kettle on when you come in the door. The ones who, afterward, are reluctant to let you leave. The people who believe, and can almost make you believe, that you are just a delight. Even though, at times, you've been told otherwise.

Once, in my late twenties, I colored and permed my hair at the same time. The unfortunate mix of chemicals resulted in a head that looked like a dandelion gone to seed - the color of no human hair, ever. Surreptitiously, people would eyeball it, trying to figure out what unnatural disaster had taken place up there. But not my Dad. On first inspection, he laid a gentle hand on my shoulder, and in all sincerity said, "I really like what you've done with your hair."

You expect to lose your parents, you are never ready to lose your siblings. But it's okay, it's fine. My two brothers were my first and most endearing friends. One was older and one was younger, a cause for alliances to be continually forged and broken. Once, the two of us convinced my little brother to eat a 'sacred' cracker. It was a Ritz, and we didn't tell him until much later that it was 'sacred' because we had anointed it with our cat's bum.

We loved to tell that story, and the sleep-over story, and the grilled cheese sandwich story, and countless more. But I'm a realist, I know that it's only the actual players who enjoy the retelling, so I cling to our memories for comfort. Each memory is linked to a different emotion: joy, sadness, acceptance.

There is no end to the ways I miss my family. But what I miss most is the natural ease we had of being together. They were my anchor, and at times, without them, I feel adrift. Even now I can't get over the audacity of them leaving me. But it's okay, it's fine.

SANCTUS
Christina Danese

Sanctus, Sanctus, Sanctus
In this advent-shrouded chapel
Site of rites baptismal nuptial funeral
Incense music incantations bounded
by arches carvings martyrs saints tapestries clerestories
Aisles link before with after behind with ahead
the living and the dead
Fringing at the ends of the stole transmogrify
becoming the loose ends of a connection lost or abandoned
Secured just enough on the one side to genuflect rise bow
murmur Our Fathers and Hail Marys
for fingers to find forehead lips heart as they were long ago taught
Pater noster, qui es in caelis

MUSIC MAN NO MORE
Jane Barstow

He doesn't sing anymore, not even Happy Birthday or Jingle Bells. The man I married and lived with for almost 50 years is gone. Singing was always central to his identity. He sang in church choirs, in glee clubs, in a cappella groups. He loved his weekly rehearsals for the Spare Parts: "vocal contractors who sing until they get it right."

Spring Sing, a massive gathering of similar groups, was the highlight of the year for a very long time. So much wonderful music, such clever and beautiful arrangements. Just three years ago he worked with a fellow member to get all their cassettes transposed onto CDs. I recently brought a few to him in the assisted living facility where he now resides but he showed no interest in listening to them. He could recognize himself in a Spare Parts group photo but had no recollection of anyone else or what the photo represented.

It's often said with respect to dementia patients that musical memory remains long after other mental facilities decline. Knowing this I worked hard at finding a singing group my husband could join once his growing cognitive impairment became impossible to ignore.

He auditioned for and was accepted into the Westerly Chorus and then the Unitarian Society of Hartford's choir, but neither turned out to be quite right. Finally, the perfect opportunity emerged for him as a second tenor in the 120-year-old Choral Club of Hartford, led by the gentlest and most compassionate of conductors. One of the basses was also a Spare Parts alumnus, and there was another member suffering from dementia. At his first Christmas concert in December of 2018, I wept to see and even hear him singing confidently and looking alert in his borrowed tuxedo. I immediately ordered him a slightly used tuxedo of his own that I anticipated his wearing for years to come. How misplaced my optimism soon proved.

At the 2019 Spring concert, he was clearly having trouble finding his place in his music folder, though he still seemed able to sing on key. By the December series of holiday concerts, he barely opened his mouth as he stared blankly out at the audience. Following the final Christmas concert, I was politely informed that he could no longer continue with the group.

These days the man who was once known for his perfect pitch neither sings nor talks. His form of dementia is defined by apathy and a lack of empathy. Music is closely connected to the emotional circuits in our brains I have come to learn. According to the non-profit organization, Music for Humanity:

>Music is an international language that transcends all boundaries and builds the invisible bridges, highways, and tunnels that connect our hearts. More music means more connections and more connections mean a better world for all of us.

A man without music, I painfully conclude, is no longer fully human.

KILLING US SOFTLY
Wendy Bradford

Ears, not quite at attention,
on guard for distractions

Eyes, with amber and honey marbling,
watch intently.

Eyebrows move up quizzically
asking?

Head tilts to the right and left,
I am surveilled.

Nostrils quietly breathe and
I am scented.

A soft sighing hum and
I am loved.

Love, training, and socialization
reversed her turbulent beginnings.

Our alliance, never effortless,
grows as a loving partnership.

Too abbreviated for me,
Our thirteen years together.

With a lump, limp, and labored breathing
her time is close.

On a precipice we stand,
awaiting death's knock.

She is my daughter, mother.
sister, friend, and confidant.

Killing us softly, me
and my faithful companion.

~~~

Amber was put to sleep on July 8th of 2020 on my front porch with the vet and his assistant. All of us masked, I hope she saw my love of her in my eyes.

MEMBER OF THE FAMILY
Eric Maynard

Rupert pulled the Mercedes into his driveway. The last rays of evening light bounced off his dashboard, decorating the front lawn. He caught a glimpse within the car's shadow as it traveled over the lawn. He saw a small figure in the grass, curled up on its side in a half-moon position.

"Oh, no," he said to himself.

Orange and white fur in a spiral traveling up its long feline tail, across its torso. Its whiskers, face, concealed by an outstretched paw, a ragged spiked tuft trapped in the Mercedes's phantom-like silhouette.

He stopped the car, staring at the motionless figure. He wondered how long it had been lying there.

He closed the car door and walked toward the fallen creature with hesitation. As he drew near, any doubt dissipated. It was Ranger.

Ranger was all done.

Rupert turned, entering the house. He deposited his laptop case next to his brown leather work shoes at the front door.

Madolyn sat in the living room. He studied Madolyn, first her and then her drink. She clutched a tall wide glass, containing a disproportionate mix of vodka with orange juice. Held the lip close to her left cheek. Rupert felt annoyed, resentful, watching Madolyn take a drink, accompanied by the television's droning soundtrack. The 54-inch television, Madolyn less than three feet from the screen. Insulated.

Madolyn turned to Rupert. "Hi, honey."

"Ranger is dead."

"What?"

"Ranger, he's dead. He's on the front lawn. He's dead."

"Wait. What?" Madolyn went to stand up. She put her drink on the side table. She grabbed the remote and pressed mute. "Are you sure?"

"It's Ranger."

Madolyn went to the living room picture window and drew back its immense curtains. She peered out at the lawn.

Her eyes cast downward: "What..." She placed one hand over her mouth. "What do you think happened?"

"Hard to say." He moved toward her. "Probably hit by a car."

"Oh, kitty," she said. Madolyn stood still. Rupert wondered if she was afraid to move. "My baby...I had no idea."

"No," he said. "Of course, you didn't."

Madolyn looked up at him. "What's that supposed to mean?"

Rupert opened his mouth to respond but said nothing. He caught himself. He did not want to get into it.

A long, paralyzed silence.

From upstairs, he heard a rumble and laughter from the far-left bedroom. His head tilted toward the upper staircase and ceiling. He listened to his daughter, Simone, open her bedroom door. Simone was laughing. Rupert's eyes followed Simone, as she made her way down the staircase, empty container of Ben and Jerry's Chunky Monkey in one hand, her cell phone in the other. Her eyes were fixed on her phone. She tapped at it, taking one more step. Laughter, tapping as she descended.

Rupert hoped she would see him standing there, to see his expression, to break her from her cellular trance.

Simone, instead, crossed the living room into the kitchen to drop her trash in the garbage can.

"Simone."

Her attention was on the family garbage.

"Simone," he said again. "I have to tell you something."

Simone left the kitchen, a gradual zigging into the living room. She gripped her phone, gaze fixed on it, tapping until she finally looked up.

"Yeah. What's up, dad?"

"I just found Ranger on the lawn. He's dead."

Simone laughed, lowering her phone. Her smile shrank, disappeared under the folds of her lips. "No, he's not."

"Ranger's dead. I think he got hit by a car...or something..."

Simone's expression turned; teeth exposed. "Are you sure it's him? It can't be...are you sure, dad?"

Rupert found Simone's reaction chilling. "Yeah," he said, cautious.

"No way it's him. Dad...He was just out there this morning. Teasing Ms. Phillips's dog. Stupid dog, barking at Ranger from over the fence...trying to get at Ranger, but never getting him...Ranger's too smart to get hit by a car. He knows better than to run out into the road...It has to be a different cat, not Ranger..."

"It's him. Take a look." Downcast, he sensed Simone blaming him for Ranger's fate.

Simone went to the picture window, next to her mother, glaring out. She was quiet for several moments, then, in a volume Rupert could scarcely hear: "Poor boy. Poor, good boy."

Madolyn turned from the window and faced Rupert. Her voice, weighed down: "I told you we should've never moved to a house so close to a busy road…"

His eyes narrowed. "I don't remember you saying that…"

Madolyn pointed a finger at him. "Yes, we did, we had that conversation. You just choose not to remember…you ignored my concerns, like you choose to ignore everything…"

"Hey, I'm not the one that didn't notice Ranger on the lawn, dead. I've been at work. You've been home all day. Why didn't you notice?"

"You know why," Madolyn said.

Rupert ignored her. "If you had stepped outside at least once today, stepped out of this goddamned sarcophagus of yours, just once, you may have seen Ranger laid out on the grass. He might have still been alive, and you could have done something for him…"

Madolyn, a near whisper: "I can't. I couldn't…and I can't."

He fought a lump forming in his throat. "You can't keep your blinders up, Madolyn. Wake up, for god sakes, wake up…"

Simone, turning to her parents, was in tears. "Stop it! Both of you! Jesus!"

Rupert stopped. He bit his bottom lip, swallowing.

Simone caught her breath. She looked back out the window, at Ranger. "I didn't know…poor boy…" Still grasping her cell phone, she ran her hands over her shoulders, trembling. Rupert could tell, she hurt all over. A hurt all too familiar to him.

He watched his wife and daughter at the window. Madolyn's mouth quivered, her eyes dry. Her fingers clenched together, tightening. Simone took a deep inhale, and sighed. He wanted to comfort them with words, with an embrace, but was unable. He had run out of words of comfort long ago.

They were silent, still, now looking at one another. Rupert was afraid to speak, to admit an empty place within himself. An empty place that he knew his wife and daughter also possessed.

He sensed a rupture, a fracture, another piece broken. Another piece gone missing.

Simone walked away from the window and put her phone in her jeans pocket. "We need to take care of this."

Rupert nodded. "Yes…I'll dig a hole. In the backyard." He thought, and asked, "Do we have something to put him in?"

Madolyn said, "There's a shoe box…"

"I'll get it." Rupert moved toward the hallway closet and opened the closet door. On hands and knees, he pushed back coats, hats, shoes, most abandoned by their owners long ago. Buried in the closet cemetery, he found a shoe box.

"This one?" he said, producing a Skechers shoe box. Madolyn said yes, but he already knew it was the one she meant.

A vacant box, once home to a pair of boy's sneakers. Size 5. Richard's sneakers. Worn by Rupert's and Madolyn's son. Worn by Simone's younger brother: Richard. Rich.

Rupert looked down at the box. He thought back, how Rich had run around in those sneakers. Rich had liked to run. Rich ran without end, it seemed. Ran around the yard, in those sneakers. Before he was taken away. Aortic dissection, the doctors had told Rupert. Such a rare thing for a boy so young.

No one noticed until it was too late. Rich was taken away.

Skechers, Size 5. Bright orange stripes.

~~~

Rupert removed a final scoop of soil from the hole. Madolyn and Simone stood beside him. They glanced down into their new cavity, illuminated by the back-porch flood light.

He felt Simone grow closer to him and his wife.

He took the shoe box from Madolyn. The three of them looked in the shoe box, at Ranger. Rich's shoe box. Ranger's new home.

THE MUGS THAT SAVED OUR MARRIAGE
Cynthia F. Davidson

Yours has the rubber handle
peeling where you cut
a notch to distinguish
between these metal mugs,
His and Hers
purchased when I
despaired that our habit
of drinking afternoon tea
could save us or the marriage.

Mine's the one with rim
dented where I threw
it down so hard
against the wooden planking
my fury drove me
to the nearest clinic
where I signed up
for therapy
first time at age sixty.
After witnessing what
alcohol did to my parents
marriage I never touch it
so we don't clink beer bottles
or wine goblets together
but tea at four was
already a tradition
instilled before we met
having both lived in London
where this Chinese brew
became a British staple.
Imagine England without
a cuppa to make
everything right
in an instant
simply by pouring

water boiling from a kettle.
That need spawned an empire.
Twenty years on these battered
mugs reflect our mettle.
Who can guess what might
have happened had I purchased
pottery or porcelain cups instead.
Our conflicts in abeyance now
our making up as rhythmic as
these mugs rising and falling
we celebrate your seventy first birthday.

WITH THIS RING
Donna Ursillo

The sea calls
Sand swirls gently
in the circle of seagrass
made from earth.

Riptides churn relentlessly.
Waves crash repeatedly
until the roar
quiets to a lull.

Inside the circle
on the sand,
my gold wedding band
glistens in the sun,
resting
between driftwood
and stone.

I leave my past
encircled on the beach,
a symbol of nevermore
lasting love.

Bewildered,
I didn't love you as
you needed to be loved.

Shattered
you couldn't
love me.

I sit for a while watching
waves lunge forward, crawl back,
tickle the circle of seagrass,
rearrange my gently kissed ring
taking away what was,
transforming what will be.

NATURE

Nipping in the air
Sudden cold grips my body
Spring delays its arrival.

Ocean blue heavens
Feathered by billowy brume
Domes eager saplings.

Bradford

Winter stole the leaves
Of these unsuspecting trees,
Breeze as thick as thieves.

Robinson

THE WILLOW TREE
Carol Maynard

"This is technically a tree," I heard the guide say. I stooped down to take a closer look at the leafy little sprig, no more than 3 cm tall. "The Rock Willow is now fully grown," she went on. This one was a stray, growing far from its brothers and sisters which dotted the landscape in clusters. Because of the Rock Willow's barky stem, it is categorized as a tree. Northern Alaska was in the middle of its growing season. The tundra was alive with flowers, vibrant deep violets, mustard yellows, reds and pinks and snowy whites. I breathe deep, wanting to take in the pristine environment, to internalize the beauty, and record it into my consciousness forever. I knew this was a once-in-a-lifetime experience.

In a few weeks, all the trees and flowers would go to seed, retreat into a frozen slumber that would last 10 and a half months. But today the delicate graceful beauties stood tall, albeit only 2 to 10 cm high, drinking in sunlight, swaying gently in a light breeze. We walked along, armed with cameras, binoculars and water bottles. The guide spotted a fox in the distance. Everyone scrambled to get a good look or a photo. Later a large hare came into view, much to the group's excitement. The brownish coat that these furry fellows donned today would soon turn solid white in preparation for the long dark winter ahead.

When I think of my trip, I contemplate the feeling of pure air, varying hues, the peaceful sights and sounds. Nature reigned in this vibrant nether region of our great country. As a nation, we have always sought out frontiers. Pioneers headed westward, seeking farmland and new opportunities. Inventors and scientists sought new ways to travel and live. We explored many regions of a continent from the east coast to west. Alaska seems to still represent the freedom and thrill of possible danger that lured the pioneers and the pilgrims. I could sense this in the people I met on my trip. I could imagine it in the wildlife that adapted to their harsh climate and thrived. It still has the feeling of a frontier, vast, relatively unexplored, calling to the adventurous among us.

I LOOKED ACROSS THE WATER
Zachary Robinson

I looked across the water. I wished I were a lighthouse, strong in my convictions, a beacon of hope.

I looked across the water. I wished I were a boat, free to wander aimlessly, not anchored to a rope.

I looked across the water. I wished I were a fish, free from worldly worries, never lost only adrift.

I looked across the water. I wished I were a gull, freely flying sunset bound, motions smooth
and swift.

None of these looked back at me, wishing they were I.

Perhaps they knew they could not be, and never question why.

WATER, WATER EVERYWHERE?
Joan Gardiner

"Water, water, everywhere, nor any drop to drink" is a line from *The Rime of the Ancient Mariner*, by Samuel Taylor Coleridge. It describes the plight of a sailor on a becalmed ship surrounded by saltwater. I wonder what someone would be thinking in this kind of scenario: frustration, desperation, resignation. This situation is similar to an unfortunate occurrence that is currently happening due to climate change. The oceans are expanding at an alarming rate. Only, it's salty water, not fit for human consumption or to water lawns and gardens. Fresh water has become a precious commodity.

Growing up in Denver, Colorado, I learned a lot about water and how precious it really is long before climate change became a serious concern. I took a Colorado geology class in college and learned about groundwater and other sources of water for Coloradoans.

The average annual precipitation for the state is only 17 inches. Most of the water available for use comes from the snow that the mountains receive each year. I learned about a compact that requires the State of Colorado to allow a certain amount of water to flow to other states. According to the Colorado Water Knowledge page of the Colorado State University website, "Colorado has numerous intrastate agreements among its stakeholders, and in terms of its interstate waters, nine interstate compacts, two Supreme Court equitable apportionment decrees, two memoranda of understandings and agreements and two international treaties govern how much water the state is entitled to use and consume." That is a wealth of information and a little too involved for me. In my mind, I always thought the law would let the State of Colorado run dry to allow other states access to the river water: frustration, desperation, resignation.

A severe drought for the State began in 1977 when I was 11 years old. I remember that in Denver, watering restrictions were put in place. If your address ended in an even number, you could water on even days and the same for odd numbers. My mom was always asking which day it was to check if we could water on that day. After I moved to New England, my sister told me they were not allowed to water at all one summer. She would go out at night to water her garden so she wouldn't get caught: frustration, desperation, obscuration.

Two years after I graduated from college, I married a Rhode Islander and moved to his home state. The first time my husband was at the sink to wash or rinse something, he turned on the water full blast. My eyes nearly bugged out of my head and I yelled at him, "That is using too much water!!" He just looked at me and said, "What's wrong? We have plenty of water." I did agree with him after living here for a time, but I am still very water conscious.

In Colorado, I was used to seeing dried up lawns and brown landscapes. In Rhode Island everything is lusher and greener. The average rainfall for the state is 42-46 inches. Some springs it feels as if it rains every day. When I would call Mom for our weekly chat, she would sometimes say, "We are finally getting some rain today." I would usually reply, "I wish it would stop raining here."

Eleven years ago, we moved to a rural area and are now on a well and septic system. I know that the trend is towards sewer systems, but I am actually okay with our setup. I take care of our septic tank and pump it out once a year. Knowing that about 60% of the water we use is returned to the ground water, I'm not as militaristic about the amount of water that is being used by my husband or children.

Six years ago, Rhode Island was in a drought situation and I noticed that the towns around us were implementing water restrictions the same as what they use in Colorado, even/odd days to water depending on your address. Since we use well water, those restrictions do not apply to us. Still, I am reluctant to take water out of the ground. I have noticed one advantage of living in New England is that we usually have at least one tropical system each summer that can dump a lot of rain on our area in a short amount of time.

As many other people start saying the same things as their parents, I feel the same relief that my Mom does when it rains. Now being on a well, whenever it rains, I am happy knowing it is getting filled up: precipitation, saturation, jubilation.

POND MUSINGS
Wendy Bradford

It happens every year in early spring as a delightful harbinger of better weather. Someone in charge has decided that the fountains in the two ponds be turned on. These are the two ponds at the core of the developments of The Village at Long Wharf and Bishop's Cove. I see them before I hear them as the windows and doors are still closed and the hum of the heating system camouflages their sound and one more thing the after-winter vegetation is still barely to be perceived. Pounding back into and out of the water around them, these Japanese fountains sing a strong and vibrant natural chant.

The fountains' application is clearly functional in its engineering, yet spiritual in its nature. Besides the sound they make, they serve to stir the elements in the ponds to avoid flotsam. Helping to renew and clean the pond water while providing nutrients to its surroundings, they serve as an environment for the fish, plants, birds, animals, and me.

At last, the outside is more tolerable, and I feel the freedom from battling the icy grip of Winter's penetrating cold. I can inhale the spring air, which warmly lubricates my creaky joints. Walking my dogs is so much more joyful and who regrets joy?

My pond is part of the common area of the development, but we, my neighbors, the ducks, geese, deer, woodchucks, many more critters and I, think of it as our own. We Aquarians, the Water Bearer sign, share a double whammy in our need for water with a physical and psychological attraction not felt by most people. My memories of staring out at the water from land and sea nourish my soul.

I read Cassie Shortsleeve's article "Why Water Really Makes Us Happier". She quotes Wallace J. Nichols, Ph.D., a marine biologist and the author of *Blue Mind*. In it, he states that almost everyone has a body of water that they consider theirs.

"The immeasurable sense of peace that we feel around water is what Nichols calls our 'blue mind' a chance to escape the hyper-connected, over-stimulated state of modern-day life, in favor of a rare moment of solitude. Research has long found that humans are pulled toward Mother Nature's blue for, in part, its restorative benefits…"

My blue mind has changed to this little pond behind my house here in Mystic. For most of my life, it was Stonington Harbor behind our home in the Borough. While not as impressive as the Atlantic Ocean, this small body of water represents possible escape from hurricane dangers, expensive repairs, high taxation, and familial memories which accent grief unrequited. The pond's insignificance has strangely become incredibly significant to me, as this ravaged heart becomes more tranquil and contented. Viewing my blue-green pond, among the windows the tree branches provide, my heart is especially grateful when it hears the fountains' chant.

SEASONAL HAIKUS

WINTER
New fluff on snow crust,
Dipper low in evening sky,
Trudging, glowing, rest.

SPRING
Dormant branches wake,
Gay profusion of color,
Some soft, some vibrant.

SUMMER
Dog days of summer,
Naked feet, and salty air,
Iced wine, barbecue.

AUTUMN
Bitter-sweet feelings,
Offer comfort and sadness,
Burnt leaves, sweater time.

Carol Maynard

SURGE
Eric Maynard

Wind gusts.
Convulsions.
Magnolia tree in the backyard, populated with pink and white blossoms,
Delicate, yet clinging.
Survival.
Thrushes, perched on shaking tree branches,
Hanging on.
A rush of air.
A swarm of leaves.
A rattle of power lines.
    Lights flicker.
    Digital clocks flash.
    It is Any Time.
    Electricity dies in the house.
    No one is awake to notice.
    No rush this hour.
        Only deceleration, downshifting.
        A sputter.
      A drip.
      Trickle down relief,
      Glacial erratics along the highway.
    Lights flicker on.

Another gust,
a whistle, a dirge.
Wings flap, another seizure,
Disconnecting,
Evicting petals from the magnolia tree.

SUMMER GUESTS
Carol Maynard

"The Martins will be here soon," I remember my mother saying. "Martins, Martins do I know them?" I thought. "Do they come from Boston, New York"? Because I had lived away from home for many years, I had not become familiar with the house guests that visited each year, coming in mid-April and fleeing, predictably, by early August. My parents clean mini-hotels and duplexes, discarding old nests, and then crank them up on poles in preparation for occupation. They come year after year in increasing numbers. First the "scouts" show up a few weeks early, checking out the area, then about thirty, forty, or fifty feathered friends would descend on my parents' backyard.

Purple Martins are in distress in these times of climate change, as are many bird types, their migration timing being confused, and paths being disrupted. But because they are a people friendly bird, there has been a long history of humans providing nesting places in proximity to their homes. Their friendliness and insect eating habits make them welcome guests. Native American tribes are believed to have hung hollow gourds for them to nest in. Colonial farmers were known to do the same. Today the practice of providing housing is popular across the eastern part of the United States and the Midwest to the point where the Martins depend on it.

I watched the birds arrive in April for the first time a few years ago. They had just completed their arduous cross continental journey from the Amazon Basin to Rhode Island. This long migration was impressive enough, exhausting to even think about. But then I watched them over the next few weeks, twittering before dawn, spending long days gathering twigs, grass, leaves, and mud to build their nests. Back and forth from the shore to the backyard they would glide. The sleek, purple-black males and brownish females created a flurry of activity. My mother would send my father to clear out the nests of any hapless Sparrows who chose one of the hotels for a nesting place. My father would do this reluctantly, muttering something about discriminatory housing.

After the gestation period, a ceaseless flow of bug gathering for the hatchlings continued through the summer days as the babies grew and gathered enough strength to fledge the nests. Watching the fledglings try their wings was a good lesson in persistence. I observe several more weeks of swooping and diving and chattering and bug gathering. The yard felt like a place of high energy and industriousness.

With the breeding of a new generation complete, the Martins were ready to make that flight once again toward their winter home in South America. Large flocks meet in preparation for the trip. The fledglings will make the journey for the first time to their home in the Southern Hemisphere. Some stragglers hang back, taking off a little later than the bulk of the flock. Soon they have all fled, leaving the yard, once again, quiet and still. A feather or an eggshell left behind always feels like a gift, and a promise to return.

OUTSMARTING COVID

Donna Ursillo

Trapped inside like the air bubble in a female Argonaut's shell,
I reach for the surface of calm, propelling forward as far as possible,
Moving in place while attempting composure,
paradoxical in our put upon "new normal" of COVID-19.

Changes happen daily, controlled by the insidious bug
altering how we eat, drink and play.
In pursuit of sanity, we chart different courses
to safely navigate confusion and concern
about newly acquired behaviors and destinies,
about a pandemic we know little about,
about adapting to a climate full of disease and fear.

Fear of the unknown. Fear of dying.
Fear of getting so sick you may wish to die.
Fear of losing what we know to be true.
Fear of losing hope.

Like the clutch of eggs secreted from the female Argonaut*,
we are itching to break away
to survive the sea of deadly unknowns,
to outsmart the frightful foe lurking in our midst.

~~~

*Argonaut octopuses are found in tropical and subtropical waters worldwide; they live in the open ocean. Unlike most octopuses, argonauts live close to the sea surface rather than on the seabed. Once the female lays her eggs, she stops eating and when her eggs hatch, she dies.

HAIKUS

Cherry tree branches
Swaying with strong gusts of spring
New buds holding on.

Deer tracks left nightly
As if to mark their presence
Leaving nibbling signs

Hope springs eternal
Forsythias burst forth in
Shocking delightment

Deb Vaillancourt

THE UPPER ROOM
Joan Gardiner

Father Joel usually ended his homilies with some advice on how to treat others or the best ways to be more spiritual. He ended his homily one Sunday by telling the congregation to find their upper room. He was referring to that place where the Apostles went after Jesus was crucified to understand what had happened and how they should move on. He specifically told us, in this room, they would regroup.

I remember that day being a beautiful summer day. The sun was shining and it wasn't too hot or humid. I had been working in my gardens, cleaning them up and pulling weeds. It seems that I spend an inordinate amount of time pulling weeds. When I was done, I went to my favorite spot in the backyard.

We have a garden bed in the middle of our backyard with two trees, a couple of flowering bushes and some perennials. I had placed a wooden glider under the maple tree and many times when I was done mowing the lawn or working in my gardens, I would sit on my glider and relax. Sitting there on that Sunday I realized, hey this is my upper room.

Unfortunately, my upper room is weather dependent. With the advance of climate change, I have been more fortunate in the number of days I can sit and reflect. Many times, I will be inside and when I look outside on a lovely day, I will turn to one of my children and say, "If you are looking for me, I'm going to my upper room." Sometimes, I will take a book with me to relax, but other times I will do just what Father Joel suggested and regroup.

Our yard is one of the things that I absolutely love about our home. Our backyard butts up to a forested area and our house is on a cul de sac. This creates a somewhat isolated feeling. When we decided to move from Warwick, Rhode Island to South Kingstown, I told everyone it was like moving from New York City to Nebraska. Although having driven through Nebraska, I think southern Rhode Island has a lot more going for it. When my 21-year-old daughter and I drove through the state on a cross country drive, she looked at me and said, "What do people do in Nebraska?" I know that isn't being fair to people of Nebraska since I'm sure they have some lovely areas and many wonderful activities.

My home is located in a rural area. There is hardly any traffic. We never hear sirens from emergency vehicles or any traffic from trucks which makes it incredibly peaceful. When my children were young they would complain about not being "where the action is." Since they are only temporary residents, I wasn't worried and we always told them that we are only minutes away from wherever they want to go.

When we had first moved, my husband and I were sitting on our deck in the back of our house and I looked at him and said, "I feel like I'm on vacation." That is the best feeling for a home.

POOL
Cynthia F. Davidson

Perhaps my love of natural pools and hot springs has something to do with growing up in Arabia, a land without a single river, above ground. As a child I watched the black tents of the Bedouins encamped along Medina road from our car window and wanted to be like them. Free to roam the dunes, rather than sit and sweat in the hot, crowded Red Sea port of Jeddah, with too many eyes upon me, a young, unveiled foreign female.

The Bedu were like the wind, following their camel, goat and sheep herds, from one watering hole to another. And because they possessed secret knowledge of where the oases were hidden, they could travel widely from well to well. At night they pitched their tents, woven from the hair of their animals, and sat beside their campfires, singing songs and telling stories beneath the blazing stars.

I liked to think their nomadic existence mirrored my expatriate one. We both had moveable homes, even if mine were walled in rented rooms. For me this implied a kinship, though I boarded jets to get from one place to another, and they rode horses or camels. My admiration for these tribal people came from how close they kept to what was real.

They knew the landscape intimately and could make their living from this wisdom. Bedu kids were not confined to classrooms or forced to learn algebra like me, who struggled with this numerical science. Their fellow Muslim, Muhammad ibn Musa Al-Khwairzmi, astronomer and polymath had invented Al-jabr. Muhammad devised this mathematical language for the purpose of 'balancing and restoring of broken parts.' In 820 AD he became the head librarian of Bagdad's House of Wisdom.

I did not dwell upon the dangers that accompanied Bedu lives until later when lost and alone, in my own life in Europe. Working in London at age twenty, in despair over the events that became thirty years of war in Lebanon, I sought the help of a psychologist found in the phonebook. He sat me in an easy chair in his book-lined study and taught me a relaxation technique; the first time in many moons I was able to find any inner peace.

"Breathe deeply and sink into yourself… Imagine where you want to be…" And that's when I found my happy place, back in the quiet, amniotic pooling waters, of some deep green psychic oasis. It has stayed at the center of me ever since.

MOMENT TO MOMENT
Al Clemence

A border of daffodils offers passage into the woods beyond.
A light frost sparkles in the morning sun.
The scene before me stirs my thoughts.
It matches in every detail the memory of many days in early spring.
Days shared, with others, days filled with loving fun.

A lane wetted by melting frost guides me through these woods.
Sunlight, filtered through emerging leaves, tinted by forsythia, colors the cool
air.
My breath forms a pale cloud around me for a moment, then disappears.
Tiny drops of water sparkle on branches waiting for the morning breeze
to set them free.
An image of someone forms at a bend in the path ahead and becomes defined,
moment to moment.

A neighbor approaches, then, pauses, hesitating briefly,
before deciding not to walk with me today.
We share a greeting, but the distance between us hides her thoughts.
The hint of a smile that communicates, before the sound of words,
is lost to the distance we stand apart.
She turns to return home. I turn to do the same.

The day has changed. It no longer fits with those long remembered.
My thoughts tumble one on another, each offering an answer to the loss I feel.
Thoughts remaining incomplete, abstractions without form, predictions
without proof.
Fear of what has happened to others, in only a moment, remains.
I have become disconnected from the past, as though it were a lie,
no longer worthy of trust.

Memories, promises meant to guide the future, have become false prophets,
images in a mirage, disappearing when approached for comfort.
The confidence of a species, chosen to stand above all others, is now
challenged.

A sense of being, binding all things one to another, has recalled me to the shared struggle, from which I can no longer claim to be exempt.
Will it be the sound and fury of worlds in collision, or neglect of the knowledge offered by Pasteur, which will presage our exit from the human stage?
Are we to be the victims of an unseen enemy for want of a path not followed? Do we have miles to go before we, forever, sleep?

THE REPLY ALLPOCALYPSE
Dyann Boudreau

An email storm, for anyone lucky enough not to know, is a tsunami of emails triggered when someone clicks "reply all" to an email that then goes out to a company's entire distribution list. So much electronic traffic is generated that the servers handling the emails overload. If there is a controversial or misdirected message in the email, it only serves to exponentially fan the flames.

I'll confess to more than a few late-night gaffs. For instance, perusing Amazon in the wee hours is how I have clicked my way to buying, over time, twenty baby Trump balloons, a six-foot plush alligator, a case of Chicken Salt, and a pair of Tater Mitts.

But my epic blunder occurred last February. It was well past midnight when scrolling through my email, I opened a message from Chaplin Mike, our office minister. The email conveyed his usual bromides of "God has a lot more grace for you than you have for yourself," and "We can find health through spiritual healing." But then, rather indelicately I thought, he wrapped up his missive with a veiled condemnation of the Affordable Care Act.

What I should have said was nothing. What I should have done was taken just one second to notice that the email was sent to the entire company's distribution list. But it was late, and I was not on my game.

I responded with what I believed to be, at that time, a tactfully constructed reply. "IMHO, the Affordable Care Act reduces costs by focusing on prevention, and losing it puts millions of people at risk of losing their healthcare coverage."

That was it, in my mind I dropped the mic and left the stage. How wrong I was. My automated counterpunch went not to the 10 people in my office but to the company's, 40,000 strong, workforce. Steadily, an electronic hurricane formed. Every response brought about because of my initial, ill-thought-out, email was delivered to every mailbox in the company.

First came the people who wanted to distance themselves as fast and as far as possible from the controversy. Each response contributed to the server's congestion.

- Remove me from this list
- I have received at least 30 emails in 20 minutes.
- Too many emails. Please get the problem under control.
- Not the place! Unsubscribe me!

Then came the Helpers, who only exacerbated the situation:
- Stop responding, you're only making the problem worse.
- Please don't respond, you are clogging up the server.
- Do not reply, every response is going to everyone.

There were people who agreed with me:
- You are so right!
- Healthcare for all!

There were Jokers:
- Please respond to this email if you want to be removed from the list.

And Yellers:
- ARE YOU SERIOUSLY THAT STUPID?
- SNOWFLAKE!

Finally, the Trolls showed up:
- I envy everyone who has never met you.
- Did you enroll in one too many drug tests?
- I want to hit you with a big bag of cancer.

It took some time but eventually, the storm quelled. Later that week, a memo was circulated cautioning employees on the irresponsibility of "replying all". Mercifully, my name was not mentioned.

Only one person at work knows my secret, that I almost took down the company's server. Matt, our IT guy figured it out. He swears that he will keep my confidence. But every so often he'll call out to me from his desk, "Hey, I'm having a little trouble here, wanna help me answer this email." He likes to see me squirm.

In the end, my "reply allpocalypse" taught me two important lessons. First, hasty and ill-considered actions, or words, can bring on a calamity. And secondly, you can't get in trouble for what you don't say.

A BODY OF WATER
Zachary Robinson

Watching waves while wandering incites remorseful wondering. Drawn to the ocean like a moth to a flame. I proposed at Stonington Point, married on Weekapaug Beach. During the divorce, I drowned less in a body of water than in a body of lies. I am still constantly returning to the water, to my past. One heals and the other exhumes tombs. Water, for me, excites my curiosity and represents the unknown. Drifting off lethargically to surging swells provides a sporadically comforting cadence. Nothing that I can do will disrupt this. It will be there tomorrow, and the day after, the same place it has always been. When the ocean is angry it lets you know, its indecision sinks ships. Its stillness graces postcards with a glasslike rigidity. Even after exiting I feel it on my skin and taste it on my lips, a reminder. A body of water that is jealous for me. She is always calling me back. I live on an island in more ways than my address suggests.

STORMS
Christina Danese

Storms have enthralled me from childhood. Early memories find me planted in front of the window in the entry of our Connecticut house, feet on the bottom shelf of the bookcase, elbows anchoring me to the top, nose pressed to the glass, watching the snow swirling just outside. I scrutinized the flakes that landed on the pane, seeking to identify their individual patterns before they melted and formed rivulets to the sill. I recall backing up to and sitting down into a plowed drift that lined our driveway, creating a throne the Snow Queen would admire. It seemed enormous, my head barely clearing the top. Other scenes emerge; of hiding with friends under the shelter of our fir forts, of turning the open treads of the back-deck stairs into a bakery from which I peddled sheets of snow as pies or cakes to my younger sister.

From the large bay window that faced our Florida backyard, I used to watch summer storms gather. Hot, bright days turned to pitch, the cloying air sulfurous. I would count between the crashes of thunder and the bolts of lightning that gashed the sky. You could set your watch by those storms, arriving, as they did, every afternoon and lasting, as they seemed to, for precisely fifteen minutes. In the aftermath, the gutters that edged our street filled with rainwater rushing towards the drains. I'd race barefoot through those troughs, water over my ankles, the passing storms soaking me with their last, heavy drops. Darkness lifted and the sun reheated the pavement, evaporating the storm evidence in wispy mists. The most striking memory from this time is of a summer day at the pool by the bay. The winds picked up and clouds rolled in. Thunder rumbled and lightning flashed as we ran for shelter. Out on the bay, I watched as it conjoined with the sky in a waterspout that was whirling and growing rapidly and heading straight for us when, as quickly as it had formed, it shrank and vanished.

During my first winter or late spring in Pennsylvania, a snowstorm was followed by an overnight ice storm. I awoke to a glass encased world of silver and white and a clear sky of the purest blue. The trees looked as if they'd been dipped in acrylic while we slept. My booted feet cracked and crunched through the iced-over snow. Light refracted off every surface, glaring. My eyes flinched and teared against the blinding brightness.

I am attracted to the power and the spectacle of storms. As they approach, I look for quiet corners near windows, settling in to watch as nature comes roaring through, listening to the wind-whipped boughs and branches, the wind-rattled windowpanes and the rising moans of the wind itself.

GREAT WATER
Deb Vaillancourt

"Michigami" meaning Great Water
Chicago's great anchor
Immense beyond words
A deep and wide blanket of blue
Glistening in the sun
Shimmering in its glory
Mitten-shaped like a handprint
On the earth
Not without its dangers
Rip currents, drownings and
Maritime disasters to name a few
Shared from west to east
By Wisconsin, Illinois,
Indiana and Michigan
Lake Superior is superior
Lake Michigan
Great Water
Undoubtedly

CAROL'S WRATH
Donna Ursillo

When seaweed smacked our living room windows, I knew the storm was getting worse. I was 15. It was August 1954. Hurricane Carol crashed into our summer home with a fury my parents and I never experienced.

Every summer since I could remember, we'd drive from upstate New York to our beach house on Atlantic Avenue, Misquamicut. We'd weathered several storms there, so we decided to stay put through this one.

But Carol's ferocity distorted that plan.

Being the oldest daughter of 5, I was the lookout. My parents listened to the radio for updates and warnings. Pattie, my 11-year-old sister, entertained our siblings, 5-year-old twins Dede and Deb, and 2-year-old Mary. Stationed at the window facing the dunes, I was amazed to see the surf pounding sand through the wild whir of screeching wind. Windows clattered. The sea was getting angrier faster than I'd ever seen before.

"Mom, Dad. Come quick!"

I'd just witnessed a giant wave crash over the dunes and up the catwalk of a house maybe 6 lots to the right of us. A second, third wave blasted the row of cottages built high up on stilts.

"This is moving fast," Dad said.

"What's that noise?" mom shouted. A fourth wave whacked the front corner of our cottage, tilting the house on its foundation. I held my breath.

"It's time to leave now." Dad said. A long-time sailor, he recognized a furious sea. Mom quickly led us to the back door. We grabbed our flannel jackets and within minutes were ready to go.

We got marching orders from Dad.

"We'll stay together, close to each other, no matter what," Dad instructed as he opened the door against the howling wind. When I felt how strong the wind was and saw we'd be wading through knee-high water, I knew I had to be brave.

Dad led the way down the steps holding on to the twins. I followed closely carrying the baby. Behind me, Mom and Pattie held hands. No one said a word. Not even Mary cried. Maybe she thought we were on a special family adventure, which we were, albeit a fight for our lives.

We pushed through flooded backyards behind rows of cottages, rain pelting us every step. With winds at our backs, we walked toward the breachway to drier ground. Our path was bumpy, full of tossed-around toys and whatever else the hurricane rearranged. I stumbled a few times. Mary giggled, probably thinking I was playing with her.

With Mary on my hip, I sloshed down to the sidewalk where I felt sure-footed. I still could see my family.

"Get back up here now," Dad yelled.

"I can walk better down here, dad," even though the water was well above my knees.

"Ahhhhhhhh!" Just then we heard mama scream.

She and my sister tripped into an uncovered cesspool from new construction. The water swept them right out of the pot as quickly as they'd stepped in it.

"That was scary, mom," Pattie quivered. She started to stop, but mama pulled her on.

"Yes, it was. We're okay. Come on. We need to catch up with Dad."

After that, we moved ahead as fast as we could. I stayed below. Soon, we got to a neighbor's house that wasn't on stilts and joined several families figuring out what to do next. Chatter went on. Pattie and I listened and tried to keep the little ones busy.

"We need to get further away from the ocean," one woman said.

"Let's get to the other side of the breachway," a guy suggested.

"Cross the saltwater pond?" someone asked.

"How …."

The baby was getting restless. I took her from the den to the living room to watch the storm. The ocean water was getting really close to our "safe" house really fast.

"Dad, come here!"

At that moment, we heard a horrible rumbling from the next room.

"Oh my God!" me and my dad said simultaneously. The ocean forced its way into the kitchen with such power the refrigerator landed in another room. After that, families left, using inner tubes or mattresses to paddle to safety.

Dad thought differently.

"We're going to climb the porch railing and get on the roof," he said firmly. We did, though we ended up floating to the housetop and hauling each other up. Dad got there first, then me. We lifted one person at a time as mom supported the kids from behind. She came up last with the baby.

Our teeth chattered, we were so wet and cold. Mary was eerily quiet, but the twins yelled and cried so loudly it was beginning to scare us all I saw mom and dad exchange looks and followed their lead to crawl closer to the girls and huddle.

"We may be here for the duration of the storm," mom mused.

Right then, the house wrenched from its foundation, thanks to a storm surge. We held on to each other with all our might and set sail. The soggy, freezing seven of us were heading to who knew where on a rooftop.

"What now…" I wondered.

"Mom, the whole house is beneath us!"

I was fascinated.

Pattie wasn't. She wept, her tears mixing with pouring rain.

"Ok. No time to waste," Dad commanded. "You girls and mom go to the lee side of the house. I'll stay windward to balance it a bit."

He was the captain.

Mom grabbed Pattie's hand, hugged her hard, then ordered us all to huddle around the baby to keep her warm.

It worked. Pattie held back tears, the twins entertained Mary, who babbled. I think she felt better under our human tent. We all did, especially when Mom snuggled beside us and kept close watch.

We floated toward the edge of the pond, all the while swept in circles from the surge and the wind. Then, swirling suddenly stopped. The house got stuck on a felled tree.

When Dad caught his breath, he simply said, "I'm praying the house doesn't break up."

"I'm praying with you," Mom replied.

And there we sat -- seven wet and weary people on a roof, in a swollen saltwater pond, rain pouring, wind howling, just shy of the breach way. We kids lost track of time. Didn't talk much because Mother Nature was noisy. We sang, played hand games when we didn't have to hold on. Mom and I traded off holding Mary. Suddenly, the sun came out -- the eye of the storm.

Twins cheered.

"This is great!" I said.

"Feels sooooo good," Pattie added.

"Dada Mawa," Mary managed.

Too quickly, the warm sun disappeared, and Carol came at us from the other direction.

"*Ohhhhh here we go again,*" I thought.

Eventually, the hurricane ran itself out. Wind died down. Rain stopped. People poured from their houses and walked the roads to see the damage. As soon as we saw people, we waved our arms above our heads, shouting, "Hello. Hello. We're stuck in the pond!"

Mom and Dad called out to people they knew and, sooner than later, we were rescued. Two lifeguards swam out to us, pushing a screen door. They took my three youngest sisters off the roof and floated them to the closest dry house at the end of Atlantic Avenue.

Strangers on land found a boat and rescued the rest of us. We went to the dry house where National Guard trucks delivered our family to Westerly hospital. Doctors kept Mary overnight for observation. She cried when we left.

Mom's eyes watered. "You'll be okay Mary. We'll be back tomorrow to take you home."

"Mom. Can we go to the beach now?" I asked.

"Not today. We'll go after we get Mary."

"Come on. Can Daddy and I go?"

"No," she repeated emphatically.

From the hospital, dad called friends, the Bowdels, who summered next door to us on Atlantic Ave. They had a winter home uptown in Westerly near the hospital, where we stayed the rest of the summer.

For me, Hurricane Carol was an adventure. I learned a lot, got scared, but especially liked how Mom, Dad, and even I, kept our family safe. I liked how friends, neighbors, strangers helped us without question. I understood the community better than ever before.

Next day, and through the rest of the summer, we went to our beach. I was thankful because I love the ocean, still do to this day. Ultimately, Mom declared, "I never want to live on the beach again. And that was that.

We sold our fixed-up house to the Bowdels. Visited there every summer. And, as luck would have it, years later, I married the Bowdels' son. We live near the ocean in Avondale; and we retell our hurricane story to our children any time they ask.

~~~

Hurricane Carol was so ferocious the National Oceanic and Atmospheric Administration retired the name for a decade after it struck. The 1954 hurricane was the first to be removed from the naming lists in the Atlantic basin. Rhode Island Gov. Dennis Roberts declared martial law and called up the National Guard to aid hard-hit areas, including Westerly, where 200 homes were swept away.

HUMANITY

Birds from Canada
Honking greetings loudly now
Beauty in the sky

They are immigrants
Beautifully flying high
Landing on the lake

The grass is green
Spring is bringing blue flowers
My heart is at rest

Bartick

HOME. LAND.
Cynthia F. Davidson

Surely, I am not the only one who feels conflicted about our US homeland when facing the American flag. Much of it has to do with how many homes I've had, in how many lands.

My first home was in a trailer, parked on the red lands of Tulsa, Oklahoma. My young parents moved there in 1955, two years after getting married, in mom's home state of Pennsylvania, where I have never lived. Dad had just gotten out of the US Navy, having done his bit on an aircraft carrier during the Korean War.

To escape his small-town life in Connecticut he joined up the weekend after his high school graduation. He dreamt of flying airplanes. And Tulsa had a flight school, so they moved to Oklahoma.

Once there, Mom worked as a ticket agent with Braniff International Airways to help make dad's dream come true. No one suspected then his love of aviation would take us overseas for decades. But it did.

Our generation of my white, Anglo-Saxon Protestant family became expatriates, reversing the narrative of our plucky immigrant ancestors. In search of economic opportunity, we flew East, to live and work in Arabia and elsewhere. I went on to live and work in eight countries, making my own homes in other lands.

Now older and returned to the US, I researched the names, Tulsa and Oklahoma. The city's name comes from a Muskogee word, Tallasi, which means "old town." In his 1969 country song, "Proud to be an Okie from Muskogee," Merle Haggard immortalized that tribe's name. When Oklahoma became a state in 1907 it took its name from the Choctaw words, okla and humma, meaning "red people." This was not so long ago. By then my grandmother was seven years old.

Pictured on the state flag, and some Oklahoma license plates, you can still see the "peace pipes" of the indigenous people. Those who carried these ceremonial pipes -some still do- shared them in good faith. Tribal chiefs sat to smoke them with the US government representatives at peace treaty signings. Every one of the 500 plus treaties native people signed has been broken by the US government.

A little more than one hundred years before my birth in 1954, over 100,000 indigenous people were robbed of their homes and lands, just in the southern part of the US. All members of the "Five Civilized Tribes," Cherokee,

Choctaw, Chickasaw, Creek (Muskogee), and Seminole, these native people had peacefully cooperated with whites settling in their traditional territories. Adaptable and entrepreneurial, they learned English and prospered. Many voluntarily converted to Christianity, attended mixed public schools, and even intermarried. But their collaboration did not save them. Under Andrew Jackson, their 'removal' to western territories was a euphemism for genocide. This Trail of Tears was official government policy from 1830 to 1850. Those who did not perish on this series of forced marches were herded onto the most useless lands out west, the ones no whites wanted.

Forbidden to leave these reservation lands, or hunt for themselves, the tribes were promised 'rations.' But the insufficient government supplies rarely arrived because most 'agents' kept or sold the goods. Many native people starved, succumbing to disease and despair. After robbing them of everything that could be taken away, oil was discovered, beneath those 'worthless' reservation lands.

What happened next in Oklahoma is worse. In the 1930s, when my parents were born, these tribes (per capita) became the world's richest people for a decade. In one year, one tribe's members took in $45 million in royalties. But the gushing oil money attracted the worst of the whites. The scale of their crimes: cheating, poisonings, and murder complete with official complicity was so egregious it triggered the founding of the Federal Bureau of Investigation. In his prize-winning 2017 book, *Killers of the Flower Moon*, David Grann recounts the sickening details.

Yet the next crime spree, by whites in Tulsa, was by all accounts "the single worst incident of racial violence in American history." The year after my grandmother won the right to vote in the US, over the Memorial Day weekend in 1921, the 'Black Wall Street' community in the Greenwood District was burnt to the ground. Six thousand black American citizens were rendered homeless and landless by the marauding white mobs. The coordinated attacks against black residents and their businesses were committed by whites deputized and armed by city officials, along with help from the National Guard.

In three days, 35 square blocks belonging to the wealthiest black community in the US were destroyed. Private aircraft were deployed to bomb Greenwood from the skies.

Local coroners were ordered not to report black casualties, so we do not know the total number killed, but a 2001 commission report estimated 150 - 300 deaths. Over 800 were injured, 183 seriously. Not a single perpetrator has ever been prosecuted. No reparations were ever made. Until

2020, this massacre was never admitted to or taught as part of Oklahoma's school curriculum.

Every piece of territory in this country harbors a haunting history. Whose home? Whose land? That pair of words are as loaded as a gun, held to someone's head, to force them from their property. Why did my ancestors flee from Europe across the treacherous Atlantic in rickety wooden ships? Was a sword held to their necks, further back in time? Unable to question them directly, I research their histories in Germany, England, France, and Scotland. The short answer is they left their homes and lands because they could and because they could not get along with their peers.

Once in the New World, they reenacted their unresolved traumas and passed along to me the wounds of intergenerational violence. Unhealed, untrustworthy, incapable of sharing resources equitably, they brutalized the people they found here and imported enslaved Africans. Ceaselessly in search of gratification, land, gold and the upper hand we have been at war for 222 years of our 244-year history, 93% of our existence.

Most native languages have no word for relocation. My Mi'kmaq friends have told me how their mothers keep them attached to their homes and lands by burying their umbilical cords in the Earth. Mine went up with the incinerator smoke, or out to sea, with the rest of the medical waste that spring day in 1954 when I came into this fractious world at the Patuxent River Naval Air station in Maryland. "Patuxent" is from the Algonquin tongue, which means "water running over loose stones."

When the American flag is raised, and I'm asked to recite the pledge of allegiance, the lump in my throat squeezes the tears from my eyes.

FORGIVENESS
Bernard "Bing" Bartick

The pain stretched as far as he could feel
Nothing ever felt so real
He prayed
But the hurt stayed
His heart was once strong and true
Instead of red, it was now blue
For he had hurt someone (unintentionally) he loved dearly
Even though he had apologized sincerely
It was not accepted
But strongly rejected
There was no gain
Only pain
Some things never get resolved
He felt that he would never be absolved
He must keep trying
Until he was dying
Then he heard a voice
You have a choice
Forgive thyself
Put your regrets on the shelf
End your strife
Just live a good life
He tried
Some of the pain died
Now the hurt only stretched for a mile
For the first time in years, he was able to smile
He forgave what he could

It felt good
Peace slowly started to enter in
No longer was there a feeling of some intrinsic sin

THIEF
Andy Rosenzweig

Why am I here? Clarence Madden asks himself. I'm not a safecracker anymore. He's left all that behind him. He still has a glow of pride though, that burns inside. I was the best at something, he thinks, no one even close. But that's a long time ago.

He gets out of the black 1979 Buick Riviera, the one with the sloping rear end, slowly, almost one tree-trunk limb at a time. He looks at the door of the club and hesitates. The dark green cracked wood window frames and door of the old storefront could use a coat of fresh paint. The only thing he enjoyed about the ride was the new car smell.

I go through that door, I'm dead meat, he says to himself. A fine misty rain envelops him. He breathes in the moist air, deeply as he can without the inhaler he uses several times a day. The rain begins to come down harder, but he just stands still. After a day at the park he finds it soothing. After a few seconds he walks through the door.

The two who brought him follow. Other men are smiling, laughing, a few backs are slapped. Clarence hesitates. He's not one to rush things. He weighs the angles, proceeds slowly and methodically. The same traits once helped make him the best at his trade.

His dark green work clothes, brown leather boots that he shines every couple of days, even though he knows they'll be coated with dirt at the end of a day in the park, make him stand out in the club.

"Clarence, thank you for coming."

The voice is all gravel, from years of giving orders to other mobsters and a three pack a day habit. The Ravenite, at 247 Mulberry Street in Little Italy is Anniello DellaCroce headquarters. "O'Neill" is the underboss of the Gambino crime family. It's been ten years since they've seen each other in Danbury federal prison. They shake hands.

"Long time, Neil."

"How you been?"

"Fine, no complaints."

"Please, sit down...Norman, couple Espressos."

A few men lean against a bar in the back, others sit at card tables. Posters of the Amalfi Coast, vivid greens and blues, maps of Sicily and Sardinia hang on the walls.

"I hear you're a mechanic."

"Used to be…elevator mechanic…now I'm with the parks."

"Make a decent living?"

"Pays pretty good," he says.

O'Neill smiles, lights a Parliament, inhales deeply. Neither of them notices the tray of espressos, a glass bowl of sugar, a couple of napkins and silver spoons arrive at the table.

"What do you call pretty good?"

"Pays the bills," Clarence said.

"How many kids you have?"

"No kids…had one a long time ago…he died."

"Minga, sorry to hear that…see my kid over there?"

He points at a stocky young man in a black silk shirt, black hair slicked back. He's got his finger, the one with a heavy gold ring shaped like a lion's head, poked into an older man's chest, jawing at him.

"Buddy, come over here, meet my friend," DellaCroce says.

Buddy DellaCroce holds up the same finger, as if to say, 'a minute.' His father frowns, looks down at the floor while he draws on his cigarette, buttons of his white shirt pulling, despite an obvious girdle of some sort that he wears beneath it.

"A fucking moron, my son… anyway, is a job coming up…would be right for someone with your skills."

"I'm retired from that."

"So, you make one exception…maybe you never have to work again, maybe."

"John, this is my friend Clarence…we were away together."

"John Gotti, nice to meet you."

"He's good people, John…like one of us."

Clarence thinking - this guy looks the part, good-looking fella, out to make his bones. No, must've already done that if he's sitting here with my old friend. Gotti's wearing ivory colored pants, a dark gray tailored jacket, with a blue open collared shirt that reminds Clarence of a fabric you'd see draped on an altar, at a mass. Tortoise shell designer sunglasses, wrap arounds, hang from his right breast pocket.

He told Grace he'd take her to the diner tonight, on 233rd and Boston Road…her idea of a night out. I gotta get out of here he thinks, least I could do is buy her dinner. She'll order the same thing, chicken Caesar salad, take her two hours to finish the damn thing, picking at it. Then a piece of apple crumb pie and coffee, always the same thing – can set your watch by Grace.

He jumps at more hissing sounds, reminds him of a bursting steam pipe, which he's seen a couple of times. Everyone in the place is laughing now and saw him jump. He grins a little, sheepishly, when he notices the steam escaping from the three-foot tall silver and brass machine. They're sitting at a small table, him, O'Neill and this guy Gotti. Clarence thinks I'll get alone with Neil a few minutes, explain things.

"It's not only I'm not in the business anymore, but my health's not so good, doctor told me last month, I got the anemia."

He glances at Gotti, thinks this guy's scary, something about him, like the two guys drove him down here, and some tall guy, dressed to the nines, looks like a Jew.

"Neil, I don't know about this…I'm kind of outta practice. Maybe you want to look for someone younger."

"Have a drink, little something help you relax, little something."

"Be the first in five years."

"That's good, that's a good thing…anyway, this job…is like riding a bike, no?"

Maybe I should have a shot or two, Clarence thinks. He's ready to jump through the window. Gotti's outside now, with a few other men, arguing. One more job then he walks away. But then he thinks, these guys are never going to trust me. As soon as he finishes the job, he gets clipped — one shot, back of the head.

He'll just tell him, no, no way he's getting involved again, not this stage of the game. Maybe he'll understand, give him a pass, for old times. Everyone's very friendly…except the two gorillas drove him down from the Bronx. Arnold and Alphonse staring at him now…like he's supposed to be scared of them.

"I'll have that drink, Neil."

DellaCroce motions to the gofer.

"Get you something?

"Jack Daniels, straight, or closest thing you got."

The warm feeling going down is so familiar. One more I'll be fine — what's the difference - I'm dead anyway I play it.

"Remember my friend, you a thief at heart…like all these boys," DellaCroce says.

A few more moments of silence, then DellaCroce smiles, an almost bemused look, as much a smile as Clarence could recall him having. Clarence responds in kind, but not the joyful expression one might expect from someone who might be making a hundred thousand, for a few hours work.

"We'll get back to you, Clarence. Give John some time to do some of the preliminary stuff, then we call you."

Two suitcases that look too large to carry, tan faux straw with dull yellow metal trim and locks sit by the apartment door. One has a couple of inches of light blue garment hanging out the front, maybe a nightgown. Clarence bends his legs, takes one in each hand and stands, handling them as if they weigh a pound or two. His old tweed overcoat is buttoned halfway up, a dark red and black plaid shirt buttoned to the top underneath. He's also wearing brown wool trousers and a dark gray fedora with a red and yellow feather in the black band.

"Let's go."

"I want to leave a note for the landlord."

"Forget that. I told ya, he's got our security deposit, will cover whatever we owe."

At the ground floor he looks behind him for a moment. Grace reaches the inner lobby door first, pulls it open and holds it for him. She's carrying her brown leather pocketbook, the one he bought her for Christmas, and a green plaid fabric shopping bag stuffed with things she says they might need on the plane. A biting wind blows causing her to turn away grimacing.

A '79 white Cadillac Eldorado limo is double parked in front. The driver opens his door, unfolds his tall frame, grabbing his black driver's hat with a shiny beak off the seat, crushing it onto his head. His salt and pepper Afro spills out the sides. He goes to the trunk, opens it, Clarence hefts both suitcases in. The driver makes a show of adjusting their position, closes the lid. The driver takes them to another building four blocks away.

"Wait here, five minutes," Clarence says. "I'm not out, go without me."

"What? What are you talking about?"

She sounds shrill, almost like Edith, Archie's wife, face contorted, a look of near panic.

"Relax, Grace. I just got to check on something, might take a little while…but maybe not. If I'm not out in five, I'll see you at the airport."

He whispers the last part. She nods yes, like always. She always does what he says. He walks back into the building, hears a door open on the second floor. He looks out at the limo, looks up the stairs, stands there deciding.

At the Port Authority, at Eighth Avenue and Forty-First Street, the limo driver takes the bags from the trunk. She's been to Manhattan, what she calls the city, maybe six times in the last ten years. She looks out at the sea of yellow cabs inching into and away from the entrance at a hundred different angles, reaching into her pocketbook for her change purse.

"That's okay madam, it's taken care of."

She shakes her head side to side, fumbling in her bag, comes out with a five-dollar bill and gives it to him, shaking his hand. She feels a weird urge, like she should hug him...but she doesn't. She struggles through the bus terminal, dragging the suitcases, stopping a few times to rest. Her wine-red wool beret matches her coat. She's glad she wore her brown boots. A loudspeaker somewhere, makes periodic announcements of buses arriving and ready to depart. She doesn't hear any of it. At the Ninth Avenue side she approaches a Checker cab.

"Kennedy airport, please."

The driver, a kind looking man who she thinks is Jewish, hoists the bags into his trunk. She gets in, adjusts her coat, pulling it down to cover her knees. The cab pulls from the curb and she looks through the rear window, half expecting to see Clarence. Then she thinks, he'll probably be at Kennedy by the time I get there. Probably. She wonders why she didn't go direct to Kennedy in the limo, but Clarence insisted. He didn't explain and she didn't argue.

He's in another yellow cab stuck in traffic on the L.I.E., the Long Island Expressway. When he left Dorothy, he didn't tell her much, just that he'd write. She'd been good to him for the last few years, in ways Grace never could. Now he's thinking of telling the driver to turn around, go back to the Bronx.

"Don't expect me back. I might be, but maybe not. Too complicated to explain right now."

"Hope you do."

"What?"

"Come back."

Tears rolled down her brown cheeks. They embraced, and he felt like crying himself. He gave her a gentle push, rubbed her cheek with the palm of his right hand and walked out to the waiting taxi.

The taxi went twenty miles an hour, sometimes coming to a stop. He thought, with Grace at least we have a chance at a new life. Back with Dorothy, I'm a dead man...and maybe her, too.

The Pan American line is impossibly long. Their flight is in forty minutes. He looks around for a ticket agent, someone he can talk to, try to move them ahead so they make the flight. He and Grace are inside gray felt ropes that form a corridor to move the passengers along like cattle, toward the three agents behind the ticket counters.

"Clarence, someone wants to see you," Arnold says.

He jumps when he hears the voice.

"You gotta be kidding me," Clarence says.

Grace Madden looks at Arnold, doesn't notice Alphonse next to her, though they're practically rubbing shoulders. The line moves, like a giant snake with its own physiology. Automatically, Clarence and Grace bend and shove their luggage along, keeping their piece of that social contract. Arnold and Alphonse make no effort to stop them.

"Let's go, buddy. We got no time to waste here, Arnold says."

Clarence looks at Arnold, turns to look at the young blond ticket agent behind the counter, realizing she's speaking to him, her voice a little impatient. He glances back and sees a Port Authority cop, a large black man, talking to Arnold and Alphonse. He recognizes their insincere smiles, from his years in the can. He hopes the cop will be okay.

"Next in line, please."

TRUTH
Deb Vaillancourt

It matters to tell the truth.
What do we believe in if there is no truth?
When did it stop being important to tell the truth?
Like Our American flag, Our freedom, Our American way
standing for truth and freedom.
Our freedom and democracy rely on this truth.
It's an American way to teach our future generations.
There is no denying truth.
It cannot be smothered or covered up
like the ocean lapping relentlessly at the shore.
Truth will seek you out.
Like trying to stuff a beach ball beneath the surface
of the water.
It cannot be done.
It will burst
to the surface
this Truth.

SEEKING ASYLUM
Katherine

Betina came alone
fled parental beatings
on foot, trucks and buses
a three-month journey
from Brazil.

Daniel came alone
fled murderers, thieves
by plane
leaving a business, wife and child
from Haiti.

Jose came in a group
left his mother and brothers
on foot
sending money home
from Guatemala.

Joanna came alone
fled genocide of family and tribe
pretending to be dead
from Rwanda.

DELIVERANCE
Mel Jolly

At a very early age, every child in my hometown neighborhood was introduced to sports in tiny backyards, on the streets, or in nearby parks. The older kids, who really were our cousins and neighbors, became the "Trainers" and "Coaches". Many of the children were "Government Housing Project" kids, meaning that their families lived in lower income housing, or as it was more commonly called: "The Project". Families often were too large for the three-bedroom homes so, overcrowded conditions were common. It wasn't unusual for there to be five or six children – girls sharing one bedroom, boys the second, and mother with her own room. The father of the children seldom lived in the same household, not that he was unknown, he just didn't spend much time in their lives. Sometimes though, the fathers would show up and join the kids when they were outside playing.

I knew I was fortunate because I never lived in "The Projects," but I certainly had friends who were not as lucky. I remember visiting playmates on many occasions, and turning on a kitchen light at night, only to see cockroaches scrambling back to their hiding places, or mice running across the floor. From these meager beginnings though, came some of Indiana's best athletes. We all went to school together, played summertime sports together, and went to church together on Sundays.

Thinking back, I wonder where the desire to succeed was born. It surely was not through efforts to emulate either single parent or two parent-based families. Maybe it grew from watching and living under harsh home life conditions: having little or no money, often being hungry, needing to wash clothes every night so as to have something clean to wear to school the next day. Or maybe it was a sense of wanting to escape the childhood way of life that was so prevalent in our hometown.

For me personally, I never could understand why my father was unable to be as successful in his job as I thought he should be; nor could I comprehend the apparent lack of respect he received. On the other hand, I clearly remember how his fortune changed when I began playing on the hometown high school basketball team. As I became recognized as a "Muncie Central Bearcat," his boss demonstrated a level of envy and admiration that resulted in a substantial boost to my father's self-esteem.

That was the second time in my father's life when he saw himself as someone important. In uniform as a World War II U.S. Army Soldier serving in the Pacific Ocean Theatre, he was "special". The significance of his military service gave him a sense of self-respect and confidence, which unfortunately diminished when he returned to his hometown. Even though he had access to the G.I. Bill of Rights, and he tried to apply himself toward self-improvement, he met the "roadblock" of resistance toward allowing colored soldiers into schools for skilled trades. The result was that he abandoned his goals, and then felt grateful to be able to settle into a minimum wage job at a foundry.

During my father's generation, sports and athletes gave the town "bragging rights". Conversations focused on boasting about the greatness of your team of choice. Athletes strived to become not simply well-trained and proficient, but skilled and memorable enough to be recognized statewide. A name that was remembered created an athlete of hero status — one who was certain to be the topic of discussion for years past high school graduation. Thus, was born the thought process that created the tradition of youngsters whose single goal for high school was to play sports and be on a team.

For the generation behind my father, emphasis continued to be placed on athletics in my hometown. It never was drilled into us that we needed to be good students; only that succeeding in sports would provide the means for life improvement. We were supposed to be great athletes, so focused on achieving fame that academics often were left behind. Athletes at risk of being academically ineligible to participate were assigned "particular classes" to ensure they would receive passing grades. Nevertheless, an enormous amount of academic talent surely was left behind due to lack of educational support — a sad consequence of misplaced emphasis in a hometown that revered athletic skill above academic achievement. Thankfully though, there were exceptions: Student Athletes — those who were able to rise above the stigma that sports and academics were independent entities, and instead understood there could be compatibility between them. I am grateful for the Deliverance!

THE EVIL THAT MEN DO
Al Clemence

Listen my children and gather near
our nation is in peril. We have much to fear.
Truth has been dealt a mighty blow.
Equal justice under law, you may never know.

Tyranny has appeared and continues to grow.
A tyrant has become a mighty foe.
What did he offer that so greatly pleased, that men their fellows would deceive?
Is the truth that lasted for two hundred years to be discarded for the gifts received?

A man has been judged above his peers.
His crimes have been denied with mighty cheers.
What reward has he promised to make it so?
Please, tell us, that we may know.

Our story began, as most stories do, with humble men, who challenged a king.
Listen closely and I shall explain the cause of this frightful thing.
From a familiar bridge in Concord Square, we still remember those, who struggled there.
From a plantation along the Potomac's banks, a general rose to lead the fight.
From a sturdy cabin by candlelight, a humble man sought to heal a nation's plight.
On fields of battle stained with blood, brave men fought to preserve a sacred right.
All men are created equal and share the gift of freedom from a tyrant's might.
Should we, now, submit a land defended by those who honored truth and justice to tyranny?
What sophistry has convinced us that others may define our liberty?
The sacred oath, the pledge we share, affirms that we may not.
Our conscience demands that we shall not.

NEW YORK STORIES, OR WE ARE ALL IN THIS TOGETHER

Phoebe Huang

Who thinks of New York City as a place to bond with the stranger on the street? My friend Diane: "Whenever I get lost in New York, no one will help me, or give me directions."

The following tells a different story.

I was running late and could fit in an hour at the Metropolitan Museum of Art, but only if I hurried. Three options were available: the subway, a taxi, or the bus. The subway was out – I would have to go to 42nd St. to catch the shuttle, then backtrack uptown. No taxis either: my favorite taxi rides were offset by taxi rides where the driver either did not know New York or deliberately took me on a joyride. Taxis were an option only when I was battle-ready with extra time. Today, it was the bus.

I jogged up Broadway to catch the cross-town bus at 78th St.

As I neared the corner, my bus stood standing two blocks to my left. I ran, probably jaywalking, wildly waving my hands to get the driver's attention. Another woman ran up beside me, calling out also: we both knew the next bus would be at least 15 minutes away. Soon, a third person joined us, a tall man whose calls and energetic hand gestures caught more attention than ours.

Miracle. The bus waited with its doors opened as we clambered up the steps. The man saw us safely aboard then said, "Have a nice day, ladies." He saluted and went on his way down the street.

On another occasion, I slid in my metro pass – nothing. I took it out, turned the card upside down and slid it back. Still nothing. A crowd of would-be passengers gathered behind me.

The bus driver pulled the card out of my hand and slid it in himself. "It's expired." As I fumbled for change, the bus driver suggested that I get off the bus to sort things out.

I turned to exit when calls rang out:

"Do you want some quarters?"

"How many quarters do you need?"

Like a deer caught in headlights, I groped for what to do. Before I could react, a young woman tapped me on the arm. "I'll use my metro card and you can repay me whatever you have." I nodded gratefully.

Recently I was in New York for my grand niece's graduation dinner.

It was pouring. A woman who had ducked into a store alcove saw me trying to flag down a cab at the corner of 53rd St and Madison. I had been trying to dodge the sideways rain for 20 minutes when she came over.

"The best place to get a cab is where people are getting out of cabs."

Only, Grand Central Station was at least 10 blocks away, and I was not about to walk there and get wetter still.

"In that case, you'd better take the Madison Avenue bus to 86th St., ask for a transfer, then take the cross-town."

In response to my "But, I don't have a token or exact change," she poured five quarters into my hand.

It gets better. I exited the bus at 86th St. "Now, I'd better grab a cab." I was only cross-town from the restaurant, and who knew when a bus would show up. When two empty cabs came my way, I started running. The cab farthest from me was flagged down by a young man. Just as I was about to get to the second cab, a woman darted out of nowhere and got into it.

I was desperate - 45 minutes late now. I knocked on the glass and asked the woman if she'd mind sharing her cab. She hesitated, then agreed. I got in next to her. A third woman then rapped on the cab window and asked if she might join us as well. Turns out she was on the Madison Avenue bus also. Lovely. Better still, the third woman was going the farthest - so she offered to take care of the fare. I handed her $5. "Is this enough?"

"Too much," she said, and handed me back $2.

A story of three women sharing camaraderie and a warm taxi on a very wet, raw night in Manhattan!

This next is not a New York story, but it does underscore the kindness of strangers and how we really are in this together.

It was 4 a.m., and I called my daughter: "Sweetie, I'm in the hospital with Dad. This may be the last time."

"I'll get on the first plane," she said.

What transpired over the next three hours was known to my son, Min, not me. She had booked an airline seat before leaving for Reagan National Airport. By the time she was in line to board, she'd already been bumped from the flight. She pleaded and explained her difficult circumstances; but the airline was adamant: the next flight or nothing. All along, she'd been on the phone with her brother, who was in the hospital with me, tearfully explaining her whereabouts and providing him updates. During one of these exchanges, another passenger walked up to her and offered his seat.

She arrived at the hospital just in time.

The Samaritan who gave Wendy his airline seat is, sadly, unknown to us. In her mental disarray, she never asked for his name so that we could properly thank him. From time to time, we think of him and silently wish him well. What would have happened without this stranger's kindness? It's too terrible to think about.

Such kindnesses incur debts that we need to pay forward. And particularly given life's fragility and unevenness, it is our privilege to do so.

FAMILY TIES
Zack Robinson

The octopus, with its slimy smooth exterior, curious tentacles, and forbidden habitat, in many ways is somewhat alien to humans. For some, myself included, the idea of a family or home carries a similar connotation. The tentacles mentioned by Dodie Smith are reminiscent of tethers that can be difficult to sever. They also speak to the sprawling nature of a family's progression.

From early on, I grew up idolizing a father whose tentacles pulled him further and further west until his habitat evolved from the Atlantic Ocean to the Pacific. Following in his fashion, I found myself transplanted from tank to tank searching for a more temperate living condition. But always close by the ocean, for an octopus has no need for dry land. Chasing treasures and mermaids from Connecticut, Florida, Washington, North Carolina, and Rhode Island. Finding comfort in the lull of the ocean, the ebbing of tides. I could never come to terms with an explanation for the sheer volume of water, much like the concept of a family.

In all of my writhing to free myself of these tentacles, I awoke a third-generation electrician, with my own broken family, for the damage is successive down the line. Although I wished to escape my family, I also longed for one of my own. But what does that even look like when our truths are based off past experiences? I have seen a lot of second and third families but am no longer willing to add to the mess.

A PERFECT STORM
Wendy Bradford

While the storm rages outdoors
within my walls, I read indoors
by an open window.
I am briefly consoled
by my perceived stronghold.

Slowly my deafened ears now hear
the enraged far and near,
rattling my consciousness
to pray that all good nations
ally with just delegations.

This World's tempest we will not escape
as death and sickness is on tape,
breaking through walls of the unaffected,
medical soldiers, multi-colored protesters
and the newly mindful turn equal rights' investors.

All together are battling the storm,
as buffeting waves form
high hills and valleys.
The engine fights the storm's pull
tossed as a rider by a bull.

Mother sea spills on our bodies
an army of tiny arrows for everybody.
To jib and main, we scurry
only a moment to make lines tight,
only a moment to hope to be right.

Safe harbor we believed found,
yet today we fear to drown
in this perfect storm
of uncertainty, pandemic, death,
prejudice, and economic un-health.

No longer can we bystanders be
to watch death by a knee.
Accept the need for evolution
or expect a revolution.
Let us grasp the perfect time
to ring liberty's chime.

AN OPPORTUNITY TO REIMAGINE THE WORLD

Cynthia F. Davidson

Imagine this is your opportunity to show us what guides your life. To keep things simple, each person is permitted only 5 pebbles to accomplish this. Can you explain the foundational first principles that support all your beliefs, with such humble tools?

First find a clear patch of ground. Sit there until you feel well grounded, for these 5 stones will be the ground rules for building a new world. Prepare yourself well for this.

Then take a very deliberate walk. Look for smooth stones that speak to you in some way. Take only the ones that want to go with you. If you pay prayerful attention and seek their silent counsel, you will discern their differences.

For each one you take, leave something in return. This is a universal law of give and take. Whether a strand of hair, a song, a pinch of tobacco or cornmeal… When receiving, we give, in turn so the Universe remains in balance. Gather rocks in a range of colors, in rough proportion size wise. Remember what these pebbles are going to represent, the rules that govern everything and everyone in the Universe once you learn them and can teach them.

When you have your handpicked pebbles, rinse them in the pond, stream or sea, and return to sit on your cleared patch of ground. Put the stones down to dry. Face North when you sit down on the ground with them. If you do not have a compass, you will make one with your stones. Which Direction did the Sun rise in? That is to your right when facing North. The Sun sets in the West, which should be to your left.

Now choose the best-proportioned, smoothest stone. Put it down in front of you to form the center. This is the lynchpin. You will use it to realign the order of everything in the Universe. It stands for Balance. Reflect on what happens to a world without Balance. Consider everything the principle of Balance means in the broadest sense. Our Sun star centers our solar system. Our planet Earth orbits it in Balance. Balancing work is dynamic. It requires you to be alert to what helps or harms it. Equanimity. Fairness. Justice.

Pick another pebble to represent Right Action. Lay it on the East side, where the Sun rises. All the better if this stone is yellow, the color of the rising Sun, the light of Enlightenment. Let this rock represent thought and intellect, informed by deep respect for Nature's grand design. Right Action comes from studying Nature's Laws.

Then your third stone, to lay in the South, nearest you. This is the sign of Trust, heart's truths deeply informed and regularly consulted. When heart and head are in agreement, human beings are not conflicted.

Your fourth stone goes to the left side. It represents dusk and your Higher Purpose, the one others mention when your light has gone out and you have gone to the Other Side. What you stood for and accomplished.

Lastly, lay down your True North stone. Set it like a star in your crown. This is for Integrity. This overarching guidance aligns and integrates all our other parts, so life unfolds in harmony with others as well as yourself.

-BIOGRAPHICAL SKETCHES

Jane Barstow
Jane is a retired professor of English and women's studies who has taught in Greece and Bulgaria as a Fulbright scholar. The author of *One Hundred Years of American Women Writing, 1848-1948*, she also has two daughters, two grandsons and a passion for the NYTimes Sunday crossword puzzle.

Bernard "Bing" Bartick
Bing is a retired award-winning history teacher who lives in North Stonington, Connecticut. Besides writing, he enjoys photography and collecting art.

Dyann Boudreau
Dyann graduated from the University of Rhode Island, where she was nominated as Gonfalonier. She shares her home in the coastal town of Narragansett with an angry cat and a duteous husband. When not reading true crime stories Dyann can be found outdoors, attending to her undisciplined garden. This is her first time in print.

Wendy Bradford
Wendy studied a year at the Institute of Political Science in Paris and graduated from Sweet Briar College in Virginia. After three decades in the finance industry, she now concentrates on the arts for creativity and balance. She lives on the edge of a pond in Mystic Connecticut where she divides her time between writing, causing mischief, and enjoying her friends and pets.

Al Clemence
Al graduated from the University of Rhode Island at a time when the world was full of possibilities. He served in the United States Army as a pilot and continued his love of flying as an airline pilot. After more than thirty-five years that literally flew by, he retired and now lives in Westerly, R.I., where he enjoys sharing stories with members of the Westerly Writers' Group.

Christina Danese
Christina Danese lives in Rhode Island with her son and their dog. Her submissions to this anthology are dedicated to the memory of her husband and champion, Renato Danese (March 1944-April 2020).

Cynthia F. Davidson
Award winning author, Cynthia F. Davidson's writing journey began in Saudi Arabia, and took her to the foreign desk at CBS News, where the writer is never supposed to be part of the story. But in 2019 she ditched those rules and published her first memoir, *The Importance of Paris*, in which she thanks "the great group of human beings in the Westerly writing group" for their warmth and encouragement.

Joan Gardiner
Joan has stated "My vision for my future was never to be an author. But after graduating with a master's in finance, all that changed after a serious automobile accident. As a survivor of a traumatic brain injury, I gave a speech at the Brain Injury Association of Rhode Island. My recovery has been deemed remarkable. I decided to write a book based on the speech in hopes of helping others that are afflicted with a similar injury."

Phoebe Huang
Phoebe held executive positions in major financial service firms. She is a Master Gardener who enjoyed creating large vegetable and flower gardens. In retirement, she now focuses on re-exploring her world through writing.

Mel Jolly
Mel is a retired U.S. Air Force Captain, having served twenty years on active duty. Following retirement, he began a second career as an educator, teaching on both high school and college levels. After retiring once again, Mel continued "teaching" while serving as a volunteer Youth Basketball Coach for a number of years in Westerly, Rhode Island. As a Veteran of Military Service, Mel currently is the Commander of the American Legion Post in Westerly.

Carol Maynard
Carol is a retired elementary school teacher who grew up in Hartford, Connecticut. She now resides in the Westerly area, living with family members and her yellow lab, Hunter. Carol joined the Westerly Writers' Group two years ago and continues to enjoy the adventure of sharing her writing with the workshop members.

Eric Maynard
Eric Maynard lives in Connecticut. When he is not busy exercising his writing obsession, Eric enjoys films, music, gardening, and raising his family with his wife.

Andy Rosenzweig
Andy is a retired policeman from the Bronx.

Joe Taylor
Joe was born in Ireland. His love of reading and writing began in primary school when a primary teacher walked his class to the library. Mr. Taylor has had a distinguished career in pharmaceuticals as well as portfolio management. He is the author of *Kayak the Mystic Waters*, a fresh and unusual guide to kayaking that is mingled with his own experiences. Mr. Taylor lives in Mystic, Connecticut

Donna Ursillo
An award-winning journalist, Donna credits a ninth-grade teacher for encouraging her to write. Throughout her varied career, she has enjoyed positions in public relations, marketing, community journalism, and freelance writing for local hospitals, newspapers and magazines in Philadelphia, PA, Connecticut and Rhode Island. She is now semi-retired and exploring poetry and other newfound genres.

Deborah Vaillancourt
Deb was born and raised in Boston, MA and received a BA in English from Boston College. She retired after a career in Human Resources. She enjoys writing fiction, non-fiction and collaborating with the Westerly Writers' Group

There are authors in this anthology not mentioned above.
Their contributions are no less important.

ACKNOWLEGEMENTS

Founders
Erik Caswell
Cynthia F. Davidson

Content Committee
Dyann Boudreau
Wendy Bradford
Christina Danese
Phoebe Huang
Eric Maynard
Donna Ursillo
Deb Vaillancourt

Library Staff Support
Bethany Kearsch
Elizabeth Matczak
Marilyn Russo
Special Thanks to Allyn Wilkinson for her time

Technical Support
Bradford Boudreau

Photographs
Czes Ferrino - Front and Back cover
Nick Fewings - Homeland p. 1
Fabrice Villard - Loss p. 49
Wendy Bradford - Nature p. 85
Robin Schreiner - Humanity p. 116
Ajay Vinoben - Boy Fishing p. 144

Most of all a heartfelt thanks to all the writers of the Westerly Writers' Group.

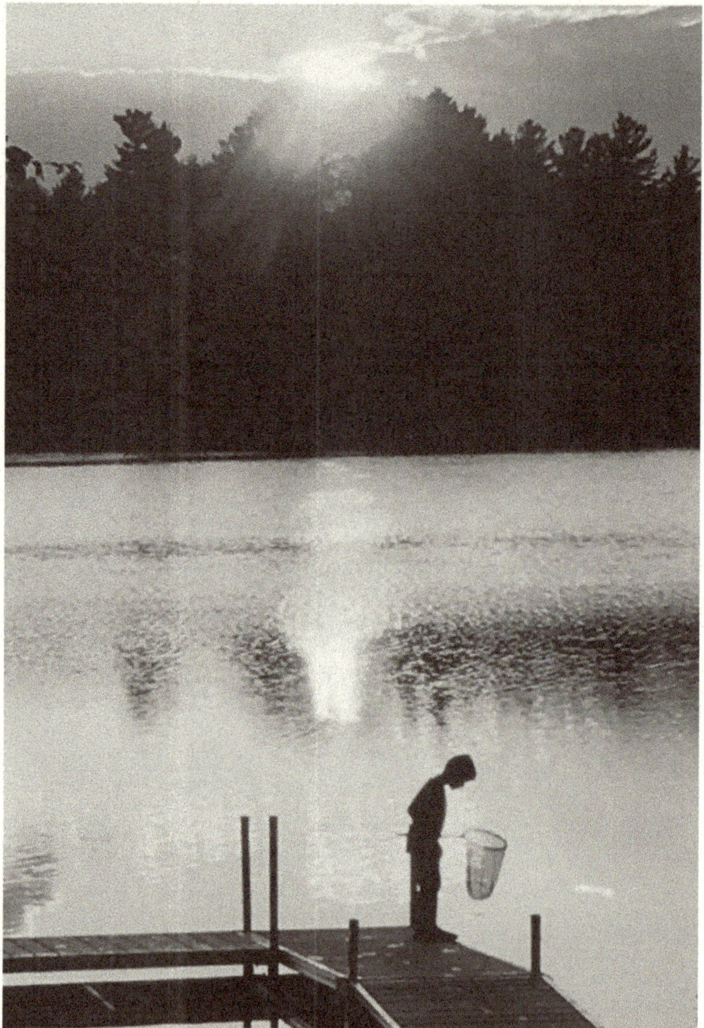